Reviews

"Bruce Bryant's work has made a useful contribution to the history of post-colonial responses to the true place of Māori in Aotearoa New Zealand. This book is a great read that constructs the history from 19th century land loss and scarcely-disguised ethnic cleansing (a smugly conscientious European could do no more than recommend "smooth[ing] down the dying pillow of the Māori race") to a reassertion of Māori energies and values in 21st century terms of information transfer and education. The tragedy that Bruce Bryant recounts, in the authentic voice of the author, has a Shakespearean cast of characters and the ironic end-twist that invariably accompanies great drama. *A Small Window*, however, is not a distillation of history: it is an exhaustive and detailed account, from an insider's point of view, of exactly how it feels to be done over, time and again, by power-mongers that appreciate the benefits of symbolic bi-culturalism but have no intention whatsoever of permitting the practical outcomes of this rhetoric to affect their grip on the levers that open and close windows of opportunity". *Beth Bowden. - A long-time observer of the uses of power on both sides of Molesworth Street.*

"Did this really happen??? Unbelievable. I wondered what it was all about". *Ex TWOA student.*

"Superb; a must read". *Richie L.*

"Kiaora e te Rangatira. Awesome matua, we have a

long way to go in this country to rid it of this greedy, imperialistic attitude that many in this country cling to. Case in point being the most recent refusal of major political parties to swear an oath of allegiance to the Treaty of Waitangi! I am a proud descendant of Hitiri Te Paerata of the battle of Orakau fame and I willingly stand with honourable people like you so as to turn the tide of this ugly tyranny". *Rangi Ahipene*

"As one of many who naively bought into the negative perceptions surrounding TWOA, we stand humbly corrected, and thankful for the courage of Dr Bryant to expose the internal workings and underhand dealings of the then, political powers-that-be. Certainly, a greater appreciation and respect for this institution and its founders. A story of pioneering in its purest form. Highly recommended - particularly in the historical context of such a major milestone in New Zealand history". *Amazon Review.*

"A detailed account of what happened when a tertiary educational institute got too big for its competitors and for its funders. Lost for ways to control the massive growth in student numbers, the government of the day resorted to a character assassination for the founder, and those associated with him, to justify their intervention into the institution's affairs. Scary stuff, well written, and a page turner". *Dr TT.*

"Kia Ora Bruce. I was Kaiwhakakahaere for a PTE at the time of the GOVT takeover of TWOA and I still to this day am absolutely dumfounded as to how such an atrocity could happen right under our noses and before the public eye! Kia kaha and good on you for shining the light on that travesty." *Grendon Te Ariki Boynton*

"Congratulations for *A Small Window - Dirty Politics*. I liked this because it has an absolute historic relevance and good source of information for us in this foreign land. I hope the message that you wished to convey may reach the masses and they can get optimum benefit from this information". *Upneet Singh*

A Small Window

By Bruce Bryant

A factual account of how a 21st century western democratically elected government wrestled for control of a major indigenous peoples educational initiative, created to redress the deprivations caused by colonial injustices; using dishonesty and intrigue to discredit the founder and the organisation to justify their actions.

The initiative is

The title of this book has been taken from an extract of an email sent by the state appointed Development Advisor on the Council of TWOA, to a Ministry of Education official on 17th December 2004. The email included the comments "just a small window to get some leverage may exist".

The levers were truly applied, and the results to the reputations of Māori, Dr Wetere and his family, and of Māori organisations generally, were left as shattered as the glass in the window on the cover of this book, and you know, those involved could not have given a damn.

ISBN 978-0-473-21934-5
ISBN 978-0-473-21935-2
ISBN 978-0-473-21936-9

Author: Bruce Bryant

Publisher: Utu-mawa-et
PO Box 14239, Panmure
Auckland, New Zealand

Email: sales@asmallwindow.com

Web: http://asmallwindow.com

First Edition

Dr Rongo H Wetere
ONZM - FNZIM
Founder of Te Wananga o Aotearoa

Contents

Images

Figures and Tables

Acknowledgements

Without the inspiration of many people, there would be no story to consider. Aotearoa Institute (AI) and Te Wānanga o Aotearoa (TWOA) are first and foremost Māori initiatives, culturally sensitive, both embodying tikanga and āhuatanga Māori principles of shared responsibilities and a commitment to educate people, irrespective of race or creed. This involved a huge amount of unpaid time by many, a lot of dipping into their own pockets to provide student resources by a few, regularly that few putting private property up as collateral for working capital.

At the forefront, were Dr Rongo Wetere and his children Susan, Kingi and William, all of Ngāti Maniapoto. They are equally talented, and have each contributed a great amount to Māori educational opportunities in Aotearoa New Zealand. Dr Wetere was the founder of the entities that provided the base from which TWOA was built, and became the first Tumuaki (CEO) of TWOA. I am hopeful that the contributions of Dr Wetere and his children will one day be recognised for what they truly are.

My sincere thanks go to the Trustees of Aotearoa Institute, who made it possible for me to put the time into the research that preceded this narrative. My heartfelt thanks also go to Professor Ian Shirley, a knowledgeable and compassionate mentor who does not mince his words; to Dr Ranginui Walker, who read every word and provided wonderful additional aspects to consider; and to William

Wetere, whose understanding of what I was writing is complete. Then there are those who read my words and by dedicated editing, help me to bring more objectivity to my often angry writing. To you all, my thanks seem inadequate.

My thanks also go to my Doctoral Supervisor, Dr Wayne Dreyer, who needed to get the accountant out of my dyslexic country self. He was totally supportive, wonderfully encouraging, and always there. Being a fellow Waikato boy no doubt helped as he understood the background, and as an educationist, he really wanted to assist in getting this story out there. I completed my doctoral thesis to the satisfaction of my examiners, and now believe that I have a duty to take the 'academic' out of that document, and tell story of TWOA as it should be told. Everything that I state here, apart from my opinions when I give them, are totally supported by documented evidence that are either held by me, or by the Waitangi Tribunal. Here it now is; accurate, blunt and forceful.

Finally and humbly, my aroha and thanks to my wonderful wife Joanna, who gave me the space, and to our children, Angel and Jesse, who provided the inspiration. Elena, Paul and Nick were also very prominent in my mind, as was my ex-journo Mum, who read everything and ticked it all, and my Dad who gave to me and all of his lucky children, the ability to know we can achieve whatever we wish in this journey called life. Words are inadequate for my wonderful family.

Introduction

Māori came to Aotearoa New Zealand around 800 AD. There is an ongoing debate as to whether Māori were the first to occupy these lands, but certainly by the early 19th century, these folk had been living in this country for over 1,000 years, and as a result developed a very close understanding of and affiliation with the land and what it provided.

From relative obscurity in the mid - 18th century, Aotearoa New Zealand's near neighbour Australia became the focus of the expansionist views of what was then called Great Britain. This country had by that time forced itself and its so called principles, socially and economically, on a large part of the world. As a result of a disagreement with the 'new' settlers of the United States (US) and the loss of its influence in that country, Great Britain was forced to find another place to send those 'criminals' whom had previously dispatched, out of sight, and out of mind, to the US. Australia's isolation and vastness provided the ideal solution, and in 1788, the 'first fleet' left Great Britain for Australia, with 1,500 men, women and children on board. Between 1788 and 1850, over 162,000 people were accorded a similar privilege.

The effects of all this alongside the insatiable desires of capitalism, introduced Aotearoa New Zealand to colonialism. The lands of the Waikato had long provided everything that Māori needed in abundance, to such an extent that by the mid 19th century, Māori virtually controlled the economy of the North Island, providing amongst other things, grains, root crops, fish, flax, flour, shipping and timber to the colonial settlers in Auckland, Australia and the Pacific. Predictably, this was not part of the settlers' script; they wanted the land and what it produced.

By 1863 nearly half a century of various methods designed by the settlers to deprive Māori of their land in Aotearoa New Zealand, had been reasonably successful from a settler point of view. As early as the late 1850s, the South Island (half of Aotearoa New Zealand's land mass) was firmly in settler hands, as was an increasing area of the North Island. In the Waikato and Taranaki, negotiations to get land ownership for the settlers, was not working for the settler government. After giving Māori an ultimatum to pledge allegiance to Queen Victoria in Great Britain, which was rejected by Māori, Governor George Grey ordered the invasion of the Taranaki and the Waikato. Under Grey, the state then confiscated, by way of the New Zealand Settlement Act 1863, nearly 500,000 hectares (1,400,000 acres) of land from Waikato Māori, and just under a million hectares in Taranaki.

The Waikato is also the name of the mighty river, which, aided by massive volcanic explosions from the Taupo region, formed the beautiful and fertile plains that rest between the Kaimai ranges to the east, and those of Pirongia to the west. The mighty Waikato took various routes on its quest to find the sea, and in doing so, spread the rich volcanic earth over many thousands of acres. Over millennia, this region grew rich with forests, whose perpetual regeneration enhanced the fertility of the soils and provided the habitat for a large variety of bird life in a mass of trees of many types, and of invaluable use to the humans that finally came to these lands. The river itself became abundant with fish and eels, as well as providing edible greens for bird life, the fish, and later, mankind.

Colonisation was, by any measure, totally destructive on the Māori population of the Waikato and Aotearoa New Zealand. Physician and politician Dr Isaac Featherston in 1856 commented that Māori were doomed to extinction and that the most Europeans could hope to do would be to "smooth down their dying pillow".

Image 1. Dr. Isaac Earl Featherston: (1813 –1876) 'a New Zealand politician, known for his advocacy for the establishment of self-government, and the importance of the provincial governments.

In 1881 the prominent scientist Alfred Newman pronounced that "the disappearance of the race is scarcely subject for much regret. They are dying out in a quick, easy way, and are being supplanted by a superior race".

Image 2. Alfred Kingcome Newman: (1849 –1924) 'Mayor of Wellington, New Zealand in 1909, and a Member of Parliament'.

Fortunately these gentlemen were wrong. Māori, having proved their 'worth' to the nation as warriors in two world wars (1914 - 1918 and 1939 - 1945), were in 1975, given the option of choosing to be voters on the Māori electoral roll or the general electoral roll. This was after a hundred years of being able to vote only in four Māori electorates of a total of 91, and to also at about this time, being allowed to drink in public houses, as their settler fellow countrymen had been doing for over a century.

By 1975 Māori were starting to be heard, were starting to reclaim what they had lost with the creation of the Waitangi Tribunal, and were starting to do things 'their way', because so-called mainstream policies clearly were not working for them. One such initiative was TWOA, a small educational facility that started in 1983 in Te Awamutu; which by 2003 was the largest tertiary educational institution in Aotearoa New Zealand in terms of equivalent full time students enrolled, profit earned and student numbers. A reputed economic research organisation said in 2003, "Wānanga's (meaning TWOA) effect on GDP is already approaching the contribution of the forestry sector, or that associated with the foreign students New Zealand takes".

As in 1863, the economic (and in this case, educational) high ground was seen by some as being held by Māori. Again negotiations to give this up were not successful for the state. So, in a repeat of colonial history, the state 'declared war' on TWOA, an action that ultimately led to the state taking control of this tertiary educational institution (TEI), the first time such an action has taken place against a TEI in Aotearoa New Zealand's history.

I was a key participant observer to 1) the way TWOA started, 2) the way it grew, 3) the way it was managed, and, 4) the way it was treated by the state. In respect of 4), I was appalled. You can make up your own mind about this, but I will explain to you how people in very high positions of power in this country used misstatements, innuendo and straight out 'damned lies', to justify reneging on a key provision of a Deed of Settlement signed by two Cabinet Ministers (as a result of a Waitangi Tribunal recommendation to the Crown), a Deed intended to redress prior actions of the state that were detrimental to Māori. The tactics used by the state, were aimed at discrediting Dr Rongo Wetere, the CEO/Tumuaki of TWOA, to the point that he would have little option other than to resign his position at TWOA. Key government players believed they had to neutralise this formidable obstacle to their plans to control, then to 'rightsize' (management speak for shrink it) and disempower TWOA.

In reality, Dr Wetere could not resign as the state wished, as to do so would have been interpreted as if he had done something that justified his resignation, and it would have, and eventually did; open TWOA up to state intervention. Dr Wetere is of Ngāti Maniapoto and as we shall see, his genealogy with its historical experiences, did not carry a great deal of trust in respect of dealings with the state. As you will learn, Dr Wetere had absolutely no reason to be guilty; in fact, quite the contrary. I will take you in detail through what the state did, how they did it, and who did it. You can judge for yourself.

I first wrote about this saga as a doctoral thesis to the satisfaction of my examiners. I now believe that I owe a duty to take the 'academic' out of the document, and tell the story as it should be; accurate, blunt and forceful.

Chapter 1 – Background - Battle lines drawn- 2004

You will learn about TWOA as you read this narrative. It is a tertiary educational institute (TEI) that grew in the small rural town of Te Awamutu, in the Waikato province of Aotearoa New Zealand. It was a Māori initiative, conceived by Māori, run by Māori, and basically for Māori in what has been described as a 'frontier town'; in an attempt to redress disparities that existed between Māori and non-Māori. These disparities were not restricted to education, but covered all social measures, and were and continue to be caused by the ravages that colonisation caused to Māori, the indigenous people of Aotearoa New Zealand.

It has been argued that Māori of the Waikato were 'hardest hit' by colonisation, particularly as a result of vast, sweeping land confiscations, but whether they were hardest hit or not, they were certainly, by any measure, hit hard. As you read in the introduction to this narrative, a politician in 1856 said in respect of Māori that "it was the duty of Europeans to 'smooth down their dying pillow"; and a prominent scientist in 1881 pronounced that "the disappearance of the race is scarcely subject for much regret. They are dying out in a quick, easy way, and are being supplanted by a superior race".

Greek mythology tells us that the phoenix had the ability to be reborn from its own, and as the story of TWOA will show you, this spirit of the phoenix took Māori of the Waikato from the dominant economic standpoint they held in 1860, and that was blasted out of them by the war machine of Great Britain in the next four years up to 1864), to be reborn in the form of TWOA. Created in 1993, by 2003 TWOA was the largest TEI in Aotearoa New Zealand in terms of student numbers, equivalent full time student or EFTS and its profit in 2003 was one half of the collective profits of the eight traditional universities in the country, who between them had enjoyed some 500 years of state funding. In 1999, TWOA had 861 EFTS (the eight universities totalled 104,341). By 2003 TWOA had 34,280 EFTS while the eight had 123,404 in total. By any measure, it became huge, and all in line with government policies of the day! Consequently it got the state's attention.

During early 2002 there was a plethora of negative press about cell phones that TWOA provided free of charge to students that enrolled in a distance learning programme. This so called 'inducement' was based on the demographics of the TWOA student base and the large number of students who were unable to attend campuses. As a result the use of cell phone technology according to TWOA's assessments, was a 'no brainer' when they were organising visits to the students. Not surprisingly, communications are an important requirement of distance learning programmes, and again not surprisingly, subsequent universal acceptance of such technology only served to prove TWOA's foresight in adopting this technology to assisting distant and remote students.

Due to its rapid growth of TWOA and the 'heat' that was apparently being felt in Wellington by such initiatives as cell phones, at the suggestion of the Labour Government Minister of Education (the Honourable Trevor Mallard) and the Labour Government Minister of Tertiary Education (the Honourable Steve Maharey), in 2002, TWOA invited Graeme McNally, to the position of Development Advisor to the TWOA Council. In this role, McNally was able to and did, attend Council meetings.

Image 3. Graeme McNally: described as 'an Independent Consultant and a former strategy, operations and finance partner with Deloitte Touche Tohmatsu in New Zealand. Prior to joining Deloitte in 1987 he had been Dean of Faculty of Commerce and a Senior Lecturer in Accounting and Finance at the University of Canterbury'. It should be noted that he is currently Chair of the Tai Poutini Polytechnic Council where Sargison is now CEO.

I wish to make it clear that McNally was appointed by the TWOA Council to assist the Council. His name was provided to Council by the Ministry of Education as a suitable candidate. He was not appointed by the Minister who already in fact had four appointees on the Council, and as a result, it was to that Council that in my opinion, he owed his fiduciary duty. McNally was said to be the Labour Government's watchdog at the Board table of TWOA, and in effect, he was a damage control mechanism for the education Ministers.

McNally was no lightweight. He was a former Dean of the Faculty of Commerce at the University of Canterbury. At the time of his appointment as TWOA Development Advisor, he was a partner at Deloitte Touche Tohmatsu in Christchurch, and was also a director of New Zealand Qualifications Authority (NZQA). It is worth noting that in the year of his appointment as Development Advisor to TWOA, McNally's alumni as a whole achieved 11,519 EFTS and a $1.45 million profit, while 'li'l ol' TWOA of 'li'l ol' Te Awamutu had 20,769 EFTS and $29.2 million of profits. All this after TWOA had been in existence for a mere nine years, compared to the University of Canterbury's reign since 1873, and an accumulation of nearly $700 million of state acquired equity over that time. Maybe there was a case for TWOA providing development advisory services to McNally's old outfit?

During the Council meeting of TWOA held in Te Awamutu on 15th December 2004, the Council was advised that if part of the proceeds of a suspensory loan that had been pledged by the state to TWOA under a Treaty of Waitangi Deed of Settlement, and was due for release some six months previously, were not received in the New Year, TWOA might need to borrow to cover a short term cash deficit.

I will discuss in detail later why TWOA faced a possible short term cash deficit in early 2005, but with the benefit of hindsight, and an understanding of the bitterness that was building up against TWOA's success at many levels, I am in no doubt that TWOA would not have put itself into this position; simply a position that it did not have to get into, and probably would not have, without the persuasions of the Secretary of Education, Howard Fancy; more on this later.

The amount of the borrowings in question was an estimated cash shortfall of approximately $4 million, less than one half of the $10 million agreed as the first instalment of the additional $20 million suspensory loan that should have been released by the state to TWOA on 1st July 2004. To put this shortfall into perspective, at the time TWOA had annual turnover of over $170 million, all from a Ministry of the Crown, assets of some $100 million, and had no borrowings.

McNally attended the Council meeting held in Te Awamutu on 15th December 2004, when the facts of the likely cash shortfall were reported. McNally was also present at several earlier Council meetings when progress regarding negotiations for the release of the first instalment of the suspensory loan, due to be paid by the state, were agenda items.

As reported to the Council, progress was frustratingly slow, but no indications had been given or reported by 15th December 2004 that a payment was not imminent; in fact, as will become clear later, TWOA had every reason to believe that at least $5 million would be released 'by Xmas' (sic).

In Aotearoa New Zealand, things very much 'go to sleep' in the commercial sector and the state apparatus as the country celebrates Christmas and New Year, with a large number of organisations closing for three or four weeks to give staff their annual leave entitlement. This time also coincides with the annual seven week school summer holidays. In effect, in many situations, it is hard to get things done for much of the period from the last week of December and the month of January. A consequence is that things not done by 15th December in any year are not likely to be done until late January at the earliest.

As reported to the Council on 15th December, the crunch time for TWOA from a cash flow point of view, was to be the 2005 New Year. In reality, however the real crunch would come in February/March/April, the time before the proceeds from new enrolments in the new academic year that commences in February (in Aotearoa New Zealand), would start being received from the Ministry of Education.

It is apparent that McNally saw an angle here as on 17th December 2004 (presumably back in Christchurch) he had an email sent on his behalf to the Manager, Tertiary

Advisory and Monitoring Unit of the Ministry of Education – TAMU (Allan Sargison) concerning TWOA. This email included the words "just a small window to get some leverage may exist".

The Oxford Dictionary describes leverage as the "power to gain influence of a person or situation", and "something to maximise advantage". The question that I ask is why would a Development Advisor to the TWOA Council, not to the state, wish to say that "just a small window to get some leverage may exist" in a communiqué to the Ministry of Education?

What did McNally mean by leverage? The leverage referred to by McNally involved the statutory requirement for a tertiary educational institution (TEI) in Aotearoa New Zealand to obtain the permission of the Secretary of Education to borrow any amount over $2.5 million. McNally was aware that should the state prevaricate over the release of the suspensory loan, TWOA would have had to seek this permission.

Not lost to McNally was the fact that if this permission was denied, then TWOA would have been placed in a position where for financial vulnerability reasons, under the provisions of the Education Act 1989, the state could intervene in the affairs of TWOA. This was the leverage to which McNally was referring.

McNally and Sargison seem from what I have researched, to be somewhat joined at the hip. I find so many instances where they are linked together both during McNally's tenure with TWOA and after; the latest being

McNally as Council Chair and Sargison as CEO of Tai Poutini Polytechnic on the West Coast of Aotearoa New Zealand.

Image 4. Allan Sargison. Manager of the Tertiary Advisory & Monitoring Unit (TAMU) at least in 2003 and presumably into 2005. Now CEO of Tai Poutini Polytechnic.

The Deloitte - TWOA relationship was an interesting one. Deloitte were TWOA's auditors from at least the time of McNally's appointment, until at least 2005. McNally was a Deloitte partner at the same time as he was Development Advisor to the TWOA Board. With a pedigree as set out above, and no doubt as member of the New Zealand Institute of Chartered Accountants (NZICA), McNally and certainly Deloitte would have been aware of the independence provisions of NZICA's *Code of Ethics* relating to audits. By no stretch of my imagination, can I see how a partner in a firm can be an advisor to the Council that firm is auditing. This in my opinion, was a serious conflict of interest, and this seems to have been belatedly acknowledged by McNally when he resigned his position at TWOA in early 2005; albeit, after at least two years in this dual role, and after he had pointed the Minister of Education to the small window that ultimately gave the state control of TWOA.

I appear to be not the only one who has difficulties with McNally's role here. The Hon Bill English, in early 2005, at the time shadow Finance Spokesman, asked "how Mallard and his officials did for two years overlooked this serious conflict of interest for Deloitte's as the auditor of the wānanga and the Crown advisor; a conflict so serious that the Auditor-General had raised it?" The rather disingenuous response from Mallard's fellow minister, the Hon Dr Michael Cullen, was that there was a "separation between the Hamilton office doing the audit and Mr McNally from the Christchurch office of Deloitte's".

As I go through this story, I find that there were clearly two sets of rules applying here, but maybe these rules only apply to mere mortals.

The obvious question of course is in whose camp was McNally? It appears clear to me that McNally had been involved in discussions regarding TWOA with Ministry officials and no doubt the two Ministers involved, Mallard and Maharey, during 2004 without McNally reporting these discussions to the Council of TWOA. It is also clear to me that McNally had 'issues' with Dr Wetere. In his now infamous email of 17th December along with his reference to leverage, McNally wrote "Rongo was very conciliatory – how could this have occurred?!! I pushed the line of impact on reputation and risk of Crown intervention – particularly if borrowing approval was required – this struck a cord (sic) with Rongo". The tone of the email is somewhat patronising and not what I would expect from a Development Advisor to a Council regarding the senior employee of that Council.

Image 5. The Honourable Trevor Mallard.

I conclude that at least the above three gentlemen, McNally, Sargison and Mallard, had prior discussions regarding TWOA, and were looking for some plan, any plan, to discredit and call into question the integrity of Dr Wetere, and to then bring into question the operations of TWOA. I believe that what will be described in this narrative, will confirm this to you.

You probably ask why? In my opinion, those in the

Ministry of Education, including their Minister (and probably the Cabinet as a whole), individually and collectively lacked the fortitude, intelligence and integrity to admit that their own government policies caused the problems (to them) of TWOA's huge growth. In 2003, I attended a meeting at parliament with Dr Wetere and TWOA's Commercial Manager, called by and attended by Ministers Mallard, Maharey and Horomia, and we were told by Mallard that "you bastards have taken $600 million of unbudgeted expenditure!"

This fact was clearly incorrect. TWOA had absorbed some $250 million of that "unbudgeted expenditure" by then; with the balance going to the rest of the sector, legitimately under the government open access policies, that had been trumpeted loudly by the both major political parties when they were introduced. Clearly, there was no budget for this expenditure, and equally clearly, the demand for tertiary education from people who had previously been disenfranchised by the earlier policies, was grossly underestimated by policy makers.

During 2004, the Education Ministers suggested reintroduction of the cap on student numbers to halt growth in the sector (an admission that they had got it wrong?). As it was only TWOA that had any significant growth, Dr Wetere correctly pointed out to the Ministers, that such an action would be discriminatory. Wānanga collectively had already won a Treaty of Waitangi case against the state on the grounds of discrimination, so this possibility would have concerned the powers that be.

However, the state is the state, with ultimate unbridled power, so perhaps our friends dusted off pages of some 160 years earlier and looked at the tactics that the promoters of the New Zealand Settlement Act 1863 got away with, and certainly caused a constructed power shift in Aotearoa New Zealand at the time; more on this in the next chapter.

The state did use its unbridled power, mercilessly, and without any compunction about the reputational damage caused to some very hardworking, highly principled people who had strived so hard to provide educational opportunities to people who until the arrival of TWOA, were effectively disenfranchised for tertiary education in Aotearoa New Zealand. This narrative will tell you how constructed this process was. Whether or not it was corrupt or an abuse of political power is a matter of interpretation, and I am offering mine.

I often wonder whether Mallard's and McNally's actions should be scrutinised by the Auditor General in the same way as Dr Wetere's were. Clearly the battle lines were being considered by the state prior to December 2004, but it was McNally who provided the state with the insight into a small window that made clear the tactics to be adopted. The results are now a matter of public record.

Chapter 2 - Déjà vu - 1863

Déjà vu in reverse actually; but so important to this story.

Remember that TWOA was a Māori initiative that commenced in what has been described as a 'frontier town' in Aotearoa New Zealand; conceived by Māori, run by Māori, and basically for Māori, in an attempt to redress disparities that existed between Māori and non-Māori. Remember also that these disparities were not restricted to education, but covered all social measures, and were and continue to be the results of the ravages that colonisation caused to Māori, the indigenous people of Aotearoa New Zealand. Also remember, that it has been argued that Māori of the Waikato were the hardest hit by the actions of colonialism, particularly as a result of vast, sweeping land confiscations.

Land confiscations? What brought these about?

After several years of doubtful practices with respect to 'relieving' Māori of their land, by 1863 the lands of the Waikato were still firmly under the ownership of Waikato Māori. There was no desire or intention by these inhabitants to give up their ancestral lands which apart from their extreme cultural importance, provided economic welfare and prospects for them. The settlers, flush with the successes of major land plundering around the world, were not of a mind to let a few niceties such as ancestral rights, or even common decency, to stand in the way of obtaining control of the highly productive lands that made up the Waikato. This called for stern measures!

In early 1863, an elaborate plan to confiscate 'rebel' land on which to establish European settlements, was drawn up by the then Premier, Alfred Domett.

Image 6. Alfred Domett: 1811 - 1887 'An English colonial statesman and poet. He was New Zealand's fourth premier.

In October 1863, he laid before the General Assembly a twelve page memo which clearly expressed his views. It would be "only just and reasonable", he said, "to take all the Waikato and Taranaki lands best suited to English settlement, and banish the rebellious tribes to the valleys and plains further up in the interior". As all good planners do, prospective military settlers had signed Government contracts specifying the terms on which they would be granted land, several months before the New Zealand Settlements Act 1863 was passed in December 1863.

On 17th July 1863 a British military force led by Lieutenant-General Cameron, with Crimean War experience and access to 12,000 troops with state of the art heavy guns, invaded the Waikato of Aotearoa New Zealand.

Image 7. General Sir Duncan Alexander Cameron, GCB: 'The Waikato campaign started in July 1863, when Cameron managed to take the Rangiriri pa and 180 prisoners by unscrupulously manipulating a flag of truce. By April 1864, the Waikato basin was largely cleared of Māori for European settlement. For the victory at Rangiriri, he received the KCB on 20 February 1864'.

This invasion ended for Waikato Māori on 2nd April 1864 at Orakau, a few miles south of Te Awamutu, when Cameron with 1,200 troops, defeated a group of 300 Māori that included representatives of at least nine iwi, and women and children, led by the famous and highly respected Maniapoto chief, Rewi Maniapoto. There are reported issues of the Brits bayoneting retreating women and children, but then again, they were rebellious tribes were they not?

Image 8. Rewi Manga Maniapoto: (1807–1894) was 'a Ngāti Maniapoto chief who led rebel Kingitanga forces during the New Zealand government Invasion of Waikato during the New Zealand Wars'.

It must be understood that the introduction of the NZSA was not an isolated incident in the history of Aotearoa New Zealand, and resulted in only a relatively small acreage of land being taken from Māori in proportion to all that preceded and followed this Act.

It should be noted that the use of personal attack by politicians against supposed foes (as you will see were directed against Dr Wetere and evidenced by a search of the New Zealand Parliamentary Debates records (Hansards), the NZ Herald archives, and Google), is not without precedent in Aotearoa New Zealand to achieve a political outcome, particularly against Māori.

New Zealand historian Michael King wrote that Sir Apirana Ngata, a 1920s Māori politician, held clear ideas of the kind of policies that were needed to lift Māori into a position of greater strength in relation to the European. King explains that Sir Apirana's policies were based on incorporating schemes that allowed consolidation of Māori land titles fragmented by inheritance. Subsequently, the consolidated title would be eligible for loan finance to make improvements that would allow (or increase) production.

In conjunction with the then Prime Minister Coates, Sir Apirana, as Minister of Native Affairs, brought about the Native Land Amendment Act and the Native Land Claims Adjustment Act. These authorised the Minister of Native Affairs to advance money for the better settlement and effective utilisation of Māori land. These policies were a major innovation in Aotearoa New Zealand, and were the first time that Parliament had agreed to make money available for this purpose to Māori land owners.

However, as King explained, the political dissatisfaction with Sir Apirana's administration led to an investigation of his department in 1934 by the Royal Commission on Native Affairs. This found no major scandals. There were, however, irregularities in expenditure and negligence in administration, which led to Sir Apirana's resignation.

Image 9. Sir Apirana Turupa Ngata: (1874 – 1950) 'A prominent New Zealand politician and lawyer. He has often been described as the foremost Māori politician to have ever served in Parliament, and is also known for his work in promoting and protecting Māori culture and language'.

As a matter of record and to put this into perspective, the land development projects involved accumulated expenditure of over £500,000. Most of this was recoverable, at a time when £7 million had been written off on the soldier settlement scheme without anything like the outcry that greeted Sir Apirana's spending. Interestingly, King noted that the political demise of Sir Apirana did not mean the scuttling of the land development projects. They were extended and consolidated by subsequent Governments, who of course took all the credit and responsibility for the projects' conception and success.

I just thought that I should share this with you. History does seem to be repeating itself, doesn't it?

Is all of this relevant to what happened to TWOA? Well, let's look.

Chapter 3 - Why the fights?

The land issue at first look seems relatively straight forward, but as I got into my research, I found that it was not quite as simple as I thought it would be. What I found was that as capitalism took a hold on the western world, means were devised to remove people from the traditional, 'common' lands that they had long occupied, to put these lands into private hands. In Great Britain, the method used were the Enclosure Acts, where suitably appointed 'ruling bodies' passed Acts that defined a parcel of land as 'enclosed', and that those living within the enclosure, must leave. I found that there were over 5,000 such laws passed from the 16th century, which displaced hundreds of thousands of people from their historically occupied lands, to a life of poverty in the rapidly growing cities. Charles Dickens captured the plight of these displaced people in graphic detail.

What I also found was that the colonisation process had exactly the same outcome as the Enclosure Acts had on the common people; but instead of removing Englishmen from their historically occupied English lands, the colonial agenda was to remove indigenous people from their historically occupied lands, for the benefit of what appeared to be the same class of Englishman that removed the common people of England from their own lands.

As we have seen, colonisation did come to Aotearoa New Zealand. It was at times brutal, but then that is what invasion and war is about. There is no need to examine and explain here how the settlers of Great Britain got to the point of using really big guns against the men, women and children of the Waikato. The reality is that capitalism made land worth killing for, and remember; obtaining it was all to do with economic domination.

Moving on from the land issue, it is important to explore the educational issues that underpinned what TWOA is all about. An understanding of the importance of knowledge as an economic factor from the time of TWOA's appearance on the scene needs to be understood in order to consider the economic and political significance of TWOA in the early 21st century.

In 1990 Toffler made his views on knowledge clear in his publication *Powershift*.

He commented:

> "Knowledge is the most democratic source of power, and makes it a continuing threat to the powerful, even as they use it to enhance their own power, and that this explains to him why every power holder, from patriarch of a family to the president of a company or the Prime Minister of a nation, wants to control the quantity, quality, and distribution of knowledge within his or her domain".

Toffler also proposed that for at least the past three hundred years, the most basic political struggle within all industrialised nations has been over the distribution of wealth. He believed that terms such as left and right, and capitalist and socialist, have all pivoted on this fundamental premise and postulated that in the future, the struggle for power would increasingly turn into a struggle over the distribution of and access to knowledge.

Image 10. Alvin Toffler: (Born 1928) Alvin Toffler predicted in *Powershift*, that where once violence and then wealth were dominant forms of power, information was now becoming the dominant power.

Toffler's comments "Prime Minister of a nation, wants to control the quantity, quality, and distribution of knowledge within his or her domain" may give an insight into why Mallard acted as he did, and it may be that the whole battle for control of TWOA was a struggle over the distribution of and access to knowledge as foreseen by Toffler.

In 2001 a New Zealand Treasury paper on *Knowledge, Capabilities and Human Capital Formation in Economic Growth* stated that several points were required to understand the implications of conceptualising human knowledge as a form of capital, and relating it in that way to economic development and growth. New Zealand Treasury proposed that:

- "Knowledge can be viewed as an intangible economic asset, but this kind of capital is even less homogeneous than is the case among tangible capital goods; each and every 'bit' of knowledge is truly unique.

- A distinction can be drawn between the kind of knowledge that is manifested in the possessor's specific capacities, or substantive 'task competences', and the kind that is reflected in more generically applicable capabilities referred to as 'procedural competences'.

- Knowledge that underlies 'task competence' and 'procedural competence' can in many instances be codified and made available as information, but there are also some types of knowledge that may underlie either task competence or procedural competence. Both forms of competence, whether narrowly task specific or generically procedural, may thus resist being fully codified, but that too reflects the balance between economic benefits and costs.

- 'Social capital' is a form of knowledge that is more a relational asset than a personal attribute possessed by individual actors. Its properties are akin to those of so-called 'public goods' enabling social capital to be concurrently shared and to resist private appropriation. It may be viewed metaphorically as a species of 'glue' holding the constituent members of society together, and so permitting them to function more productively in the economic sphere. Social capital must be constructed jointly through direct human interaction, whereas such is not necessarily the case for other forms of human capital".

From literature examined for my thesis, it is apparent that capital had transformed over the 20th century to a situation where knowledge had become a very important aspect of capital and capitalism. As a consequence, both internationally and in Aotearoa New Zealand, access to knowledge had become an important economic factor in the late 20th century. In the early 21st century there were numerous studies that linked education to economic growth, and further, that there appeared to be little doubt that some secondary and tertiary education in life was important for individuals.

The New Zealand Waitangi Tribunal rulings of 1999 relating to wānanga, referred to the importance of learning to Māori, and of the duty of the state to protect Māori interests. In 2000, the New Zealand Ministry of Research, Science and Technology proposed that the Government, amongst other things, should ensure that investment in education be made to enable all students, particularly Māori and Pacific island students, to develop the skills needed to participate in a knowledge society.

In 2001, the New Zealand Treasury referred to the over-representation of Māori and Pacific people amongst those with low skills, which resulted in social fragmentation to the extent that it was unfairly disadvantaging them. Treasury postulated that there was more scope to increase average years of education, to directly improve well-being, by focusing attention on the twenty percent of young people of Aotearoa New Zealand who leave school without recognised qualifications, a category that Māori were overrepresented in.

The Waitangi Tribunal noted that the introduction of wānanga into the tertiary education sector as a result of the Education Amendment Act 1990 opened the way for previously established Māori education providers to apply for tertiary status. This was presumably an acknowledgment that Māori might achieve better educational outcomes if they learnt in an environment of āhuatanga Māori according to tikanga Māori that TEI wānanga, by statute, were set up to provide.

Critical to this story is the fact that in 1998, the NZ National Party-led Government announced that the cap on student numbers would be lifted in 1999, a policy that was adopted and continued by the incoming NZ Labour Party-led Government in 1999. This cap was a ceiling mechanism that had long been in place restrict and control growth in the sector, and was, at the time, around 2% annual increase in student numbers. The lifting of the cap meant that any student who enrolled in a TEI course that had previously been approved by the New Zealand Qualifications Authority (NZQA) as to quality, and newly formed Tertiary Education Commission (TEC) as to relevance, then the TEI would be paid the appropriate EFTS value for the student enrolment by the Ministry of Education.

The above tells us that by 1998 (five years after TWOA was created) both major political parties in government seemed to have embraced the 'knowledge wave' economy that was the international flavour of the time, and endorsed this by making it possible for any student who wished to enrol in an Aotearoa New Zealand TEI, subject to the qualifications related above, to do so.

The NZ Labour Party led Government's *Tertiary Education Strategy for 2002-07* released prior to or early in 2002, stated that the policies that they put in place would result in a stronger emphasis on increasing Māori participation in higher education. This objective appeared to have been at the core of tertiary education strategies of both Governments in Aotearoa New Zealand in the last decade on the 20th century.

Reports on these strategies confirm that TWOA was extremely successful in increasing participation in higher education generally and to Māori in particular. So why then, give TWOA 'the bash'? May it have had something to do with Toffler's views relating Prime Ministers of a nation, wanting to control the quantity, quality, and distribution of knowledge within his or her domain?

Chapter 4 – TWOA

One hundred and thirty years after the introduction of the NZSA, three wānanga - tertiary educational institutions were created as a result of the provisions of the Education Amendment Act of 1990. This Act was described by the then Minister of Education, Honourable Phil Goff, as "the most significant reform ever carried out in the history of the New Zealand system of tertiary education and training". Essentially the Act gave to three wānanga, similar status, that is, tertiary educational institutional status (TEIs) to that of universities, polytechnics and colleges of education. The wānanga, (Te Wānanga o Aotearoa, Te Whare Wānanga o Awanuiārangi and Te Wānanga-o-Raukawa) were therefore afforded all privileges and rights of these institutions.

The definition of wānanga in the Act gave them the special function to assist the application of knowledge regarding āhuatanga Māori (Māori tradition), according to tikanga Māori (Māori custom). It must be noted that the same Act that introduced wānanga to the definition of TEIs also introduced the provision that capital funding would no longer be provided to TEIs, including new TEIs. Therefore the three wānanga that were established - the only new TEIs since the introduction of the Act, were unable to get capital funding from the state, although the rest of the sector had received hundreds of millions of state funding, over many decades.

TWOA grew from an initiative that had a long history of struggle from very basic beginnings. Dr Rongo Wetere conceived the idea that became TWOA in 1983 following a successful initiative to build a marae at Te Awamutu College. For this initial project contributions were made by expelled and unemployed former students of that college. This led to the first incarnation of TWOA, the Waipa Kōkiri Arts Centre. As a last resort this centre was built on the site of the rubbish tip of Te Awamutu College, since opposition from local residents to having a 'Māori organisation' in their backyard, had foiled plans to build on other sites.

Te Awamutu in 1897.

Image 11. Te Awamutu: 1897 – 33 years after Orakau

Now remember, Te Awamutu was a 'frontier' town; a centre from which the military set out in 1863 to end the 'land wars'; a centre of extreme affluence generated from the rich farming land owned by settler families who took over the confiscated lands from Māori after the land wars. Putting it bluntly, Te Awamutu had many of the characteristics of a red neck town and all that this implies. In this town the sad truth was that Māori did not really have a place. No wonder Dr Wetere had so much trouble locating his centre, due to constant protests regarding having a Māori organisation in 'our' neighbourhood.

Image 12. Te Awamutu: recent times.

By 1988, the Waipa Kōkiri Arts Centre was offering a wider range of courses and had changed its status to Aotearoa Institute - Te Kuratini o Nga Waka Trust Board (Aotearoa Institute or AI), and had become a charitable trust "committed to the furtherance of Māori participation in, and access to, education".

In 1993 wānanga status was granted to AI by Gazette Notice, but, as a charitable trust, it did not meet the statutory requirements for a TEI. As a result of this, and acting on advice received from representatives of the Ministry of Education, a new entity, TWOA was created in that year. This new entity assumed at no cost the infrastructure, the operations and staff, and the use free of charge (at that stage), of all of AI's assets. Additionally, and with the full knowledge of the Ministry of Education, all the Trustees of the AI became Councillors of TWOA.

This TEI status qualified the three wānanga for Ministry of Education tertiary education funding and entitled TWOA to receive equivalent full times student (EFTS) funding, in line with the universities, polytechnics and colleges of education. The basis of the calculation of EFTS value was Treasury driven, and in general terms, was calculated to provide approximately 85% as a contribution to the costs of delivery of the course by the TEI to the student, and 15% as a capital maintenance contribution.

This capital maintenance contribution, therefore assumed that a TEI had a capital base to maintain. This was not lost on the newly created wānanga, who were created by an Act that denied new TEI's (wānanga) the rights to state provided capital funding. We will return to this critical issue later, but at this stage, let's follow the progress of TWOA.

By 1998 TWOA was operating from campuses in Hamilton, Mangere, Ngā Tapuwae Community Centre in Manukau City, Porirua, Rotorua, Te Awamutu and Te Kuiti. With the exception of the Ngā Tapuwae facility, all the campuses were owned by AI, and were made available to TWOA, initially at no cost. In 1998, TWOA had 103.7

equivalent full time staff; total revenues of $4.3 million; a surplus of $49,939; $159,059 invested in buildings and net assets per student of $728 at 31st December 1998. By way of comparison, at the same date, the University of Auckland had net assets per student of $23,809.

By the end of 2003, TWOA had become the largest TEI in Aotearoa New Zealand in terms of EFTS, student numbers and profit. TWOA outperformed all other TEIs on all counts because students, of their own accord, enrolled in courses offered by TWOA. The student number growth at TWOA is shown in Figure 1 on page 192, and totalled 66,000. By 2003, TWOA had total revenues of $187 million and a surplus of $33 million. This surplus was just under one half of the total surpluses of the eight universities in Aotearoa New Zealand for that year.

Included in the calculation of the 2003 surplus earned by TWOA, were student fees of $3 million, whereas the surpluses for the eight universities took into account total student fees of $584 million. The average student fee for TWOA students in 2003 was $52, compared to $3,460 per student for those who attended the eight universities in that year. I believe that a lot of this was paid by the state through the student loan scheme. TWOA was clearly an extremely successful business model.

On page 192 are graphs that visually demonstrate the growth in student numbers and EFTS at TWOA between 1998 and 2005. These are figures 1 and 2.

TWOA was very successful in attracting to tertiary education people who had not previously been part of the sector. Remember, this was only possible due to the uncapped funding policies introduced by the NZ National Party Government in 1990, later adopted and refined by the NZ Labour-led Government; solely adopted to increase participation in the sector, as a matter of economic priority. This point must not be lost, and it must be understood that the 'open access' policies grew out of the international acceptance of the knowledge wave, and of the importance of a knowledge economy to a country's development in the later decades of the 20th century.

Students who enrolled at TWOA did not necessarily affect the enrolment numbers of the other universities of Aotearoa New Zealand, due to the type of courses offered by TWOA, which initially focused on foundation courses and those relating to work preparedness (Mahi Ora) and Māori language (Te Ara Reo). However, there is little doubt that the amount of public funding that was being brought to TWOA by the student enrolments, certainly affected these universities. This apparently unbudgeted funding that went to TWOA was seen by many to distort the sector in a significant way, and we saw on page 30 that Mallard reckoned that “bastards” at TWOA were responsible for this apparent budget blow out.

TWOA provided high quality facilities, resources and attention to its students, employing over 300 kaitiaki (guardians) to provide support to students, often in the students’ homes. The quality of courses offered by TWOA was never questioned during the process to discredit TWOA, although there was frequent innuendo regarding 'substandard courses' offered by other institutions, which were attributed to TWOA.

There was a lot published in 2004 about courses such as 'hip hop', and although such courses were provided, TWOA never ran any such programmes. It was the clear directive and edict of the Tumuaki, Dr Wetere, that TWOA would only offer courses that added academic or work skills to a student, and that it would not demean the students, by doing otherwise.

Dr Ranginui Walker was a member of the NZQA and he had a lot to do with TWOA in that role. As a much respected and highly regarded Māori academic, there would not be many people better placed to carry out quality control exercises of TWOA deliverables. Dr Walker has a book due out later in 2012 in which he will dispel any doubts anyone could have regarding the quality of all courses offered by TWOA.

Chapter 5 – TWOA rankings in the sector

In order to understand why TWOA became a problem to the state, it has to be understood where TWOA was ranked in the sector up to 2004. This chapter will look at the financial results of a segment of the tertiary education sector in Aotearoa New Zealand. To do this, figures of TEIs that came under the definition of universities in the Education Amendment Act 1990 were examined, and those defined as polytechnics and colleges of education, excluded. It was not intended to diminish or dismiss the importance of polytechnics and colleges of education in the sector, but rather to highlight the relevance of TWOA by comparison with a smaller specific part of the sector, being those defined as universities under that Act.

The detailed analysis of the financial results of the eight universities in Aotearoa New Zealand that was carried out, and compared to the results of TWOA. The purpose was to show the relevance or otherwise of TWOA to the tertiary education sector in the time frame 1998 to 2004. The financial data analysed was based entirely on information taken from the published, audited annual reports of the selected entities. This information is in the public domain, and as each of the financial reports had been completed to the same accounting standards required by statute, comparisons are considered to be reliable.

It was in an environment of a "commitment to tertiary

education", the "raising of foundation skills" and the adoption of strategies that assisted "to contribute to achievement of Māori development aspirations", that TWOA entered the tertiary education sector. The examination was therefore designed to show whether there were increases in participation in the sector, particularly by those TEIs providing for Māori aspirations, and providing for the raising of foundation skills, and who delivered on these key objectives.

The time period selected for the financial comparison model (1998 - 2003) was done for the following reasons:

1) In 1998, TWOA had 920 students, and EFTS of 693. This is less than 0.76% of the total student numbers and EFTS of the eight universities that was used in the comparison model.
2) The NZ Labour Party-led Government, so critical to the events of 2004 and 2005, was elected to power in November 1999.
3) In 1999, the cap on TEI student numbers was lifted, meaning that every student was funded for an approved course of study at a TEI.
4) By 2003, TWOA had 63,387 students and 34,280 EFTS.

A financial analysis of TWOA alone would not have had a great deal of significance, as it is only by comparison with peers in the sector, that the relevance of TWOA could be seen. The financial data analysed also provided a platform from which the financial issues that were central to the state's case against TWOA in 2005, were able to be put into context and understood.

In essence, the Education Amendment Act 1990 paved the way for Māori tertiary educational institutions, and the 2002 Tertiary Education Strategy document set out what the NZ Labour-led Government wished all TEIs including wānanga, to achieve. During the period under review, funding of TEIs was both public and private; by way of state provided EFTS funding (public) and by way of student fees (private), which came both from Aotearoa New Zealand and overseas students.

To reiterate, EFTS funding is based on a set amount payable to the TEI by the state for each student who enrolled for a course of study. There are safeguards as to what constitutes an enrolment, and generally this process is very well audited. The amount funded for each course of study varies according to the calculated cost of delivery of the course and this variation is in the range of $5,000 to $15,000. A course can also be allocated by half-EFTS; an example being six month courses, or a part time course of study. This is the reason why TEIs student numbers often exceed EFTS.

Student fees are a significant part of the revenues of TEIs generally. In 2002 the NZ Labour-led Government wished to have an eighty twenty (80/20) funding ratio between public (EFTS) and private funding. This means, for every dollar of state provided funding (EFTS); the student should contribute twenty cents to the TEI by way of student fees. It should be understood that a high portion of the student fees received by TEIs are as a result of students borrowing from the state under the student loan scheme.

According to the *Financial Statements of the Government of New Zealand for the Six Months Ended 31 December 2005. – 17 February 2006*, at 31st December 2004, the total amount of state debt as a result of student loans, was $6.1 billion. I think it would be fair to say that at the very most $15 million of this massive state asset would have been paid to TWOA students, because a principal objective of TWOA was to not charge student fees. As you will see in 2003, of $187 million total revenues earned by TWOA, only $3.3 million was from student fees. It is worth noting, in that year, the eight universities received just on half a billion dollars of student fees - $500 million!

The selected sector as a whole during the period under review was reflected by using EFTS numbers, EFTS value, student numbers and student fees received. Student fees normally would not be considered as part of a growth analysis statistic, however I am arguing that the inclusion of these figures is relevant from a comparative perspective due to the virtual nil fee policy of TWOA, and that this should be taken into account when judgements relating to the financial position of TWOA, are considered.

The analysis was based on information contained in the audited, published Annual Reports of the TEIs and were classified for University of Auckland, Auckland University of Technology (AUT), University of Canterbury, Lincoln University, Massey University, University of Otago, Victoria University, and Waikato University, with TWOA shown separately.

In **1998**, the sector as described is set out in Table 1 on page 195.

Key observations from Table 1

- There were 102,369 EFTS and 143,273 students enrolled in the eight universities in this year.
- Student fees paid to the eight universities were $293 million, or 43.4% of Government funded EFTS funding received.
- There were 693 EFTS and 920 students enrolled in TWOA in this year.
- Student fees paid to TWOA were $843,000, or 26.9% of Government funded EFTS funding received.

Summary:

- TWOA was an insignificant player in the sector during this year.

In **2001,** three years later, the year of the Deed of Settlement (more about this later) was signed by the Crown and TWOA and that initiated the release of capital funding to TWOA in the 2002 calendar year. The results for this year are recorded in Table 2 on page 196.

Key observations from Table 2

- There were 106,220 EFTS (1998, 102,369) and 152,555 students enrolled in the eight universities in this year (1998: 143,273).
- Student Fees paid to the eight universities were

$406 million (1998: $293 million), or 62.8% (1998: 43.4%) of Government funded EFTS funding received.

- There were 6,118 EFTS (1998: 693) and 16,423 students (1998: 920) enrolled in TWOA in this year.
- Student Fees paid to TWOA were $5.6 million (1998: $843,000), or 18.6% (1998: 26.9%) of Government funded EFTS funding received.

Summary:

- The eight universities EFTS increased by 3,852 or 3.7% and student numbers increased by 9,282, or 6.47%.
- TWOA EFTS increased by 5,425, compared with the 3,852 for the eight universities in the same period, and student numbers by 15,503, compared with 9,282 for the eight universities. Percentage increases for TWOA, have not been included; they are obviously extreme and well into the hundreds.

In **2003**, two years advanced from the 2001 analysis, and five years since the 1998 analysis, and is the year when TWOA achieved more EFTS and more student numbers than any other TEI in Aotearoa New Zealand. The results for this year are recorded in Table 3 on page 197.

Key observations from Table 3

- There were 123,404 EFTS numbers (2001: 106,220) and 169,005 students enrolled (2001:

152,555) in the eight universities in this year.

- Student fees paid to the eight universities were $584 million (2001: $406 million), or 74.8% (2001: 62.8%) of Government funded EFTS funding received.
- There were 34,280 EFTS numbers (2001: 6,118 EFTS) and 63,387 students enrolled (2001: 16,423) in TWOA in this year.
- Student fees paid to TWOA were $3.3 million (2001: $5.6 million), or 0.6% (2001: 18.6%) of Government funded EFTS funding received.

Summary:

- Between 2001 and 2003, the eight universities EFTS increased by 7,184 or 5.82% and student numbers increased by 16,450, or 10.8%.
- Between 2001 and 2003, TWOA EFTS increased by 28,162 or 460.3%, and student numbers by 46,964 or 286%.

Graphs were prepared to emphasise the rapid increase in TWOA's impact on the sector, and these are Figures 3, 4 and 5 on pages 193 and 194.

Figure 3 showed the total student fees by dollar value received by the eight universities and TWOA in total; that for the eight universities (both represented by the top line) and that for TWOA (shown as the bottom line). In TWOA's case, the student fees received barely register on the graph and as a result the total line and that of the eight universities line, are almost one and the same.

Figure 4 shows the total EFTS funding by dollar value received by the eight universities (the top line) and that for TWOA (the bottom line). It was noted that the line representing the eight universities, was relatively flat for 1998, 1999 and 2000, then dipped slightly, before increasing quite significantly after 2001. TWOA showed a consistent and rapid rise from 1998.

Figure 5 shows the total EFTS attributed to the eight universities and TWOA in total (the top line); that for the eight universities (the middle line) and that for TWOA (the bottom line). Figure 5 also shows that the TWOA accounted for most of EFTS growth in the selected sector in 2003.

Figure 6 on page 194 shows the total student numbers enrolled by eight universities and TWOA in total (the top line); that for the eight universities (the middle line) and that for TWOA (the bottom line). Note that TWOA accounted for most of the increase. Figure 6 also shows that the participation increases in the eight Universities of Aotearoa New Zealand were not dramatic between 1998 and 2003, as is shown by the middle line. Against this is the steep increase in the incline of TWOA with the bottom line, which consequently resulted in the steep incline in the total student number line.

For the sake of clarity, Table 3 on page 197, shows that by the end of 2003, TWOA consumed $177 million of state funded EFTS, compared to $191 million consumed by the University of Auckland, and that TWOA accounted for 18.46% of all EFTS funding paid by the state to the group under review. At 34,280 EFTS for 2003, compared to the 27,205 of the University of Auckland, TWOA's share of state funded EFTS numbers was 22.64% of the total of the nine TEIs that comprise the group under review. The fact that TWOA had more EFTS than the University of Auckland, but received a smaller dollar amount from the state is a reflection of the different type of courses, and therefore EFTS value, offered by the two TEIs.

Table 4 on page 198 shows a six year progression from 1998 to 2003 of the total statistics of the eight universities, compared to those of TWOA.

The significance of TWOA and its size in terms of EFTS funding, net surplus for the year, EFTS and student numbers is demonstrated by the data summary in Table 5.

Table 5: Data Summary 2003 ($, 000)

2003	EFTS $	S fees $	Surplus $	EFTS #	Student #
Total Unis	$782,023	$584,815	$71,761	123,404	169,005
SF to EFT		74.80%			
TWOA	$177,026	$3,304	$33,247	34,280	63,387
TWOA	22.64%	0.56%	46.33%	27.78%	37.51%
Group Total	$959,049	$588,119	$105,008	157,684	232,392
TWOA	18.46%	0.56%	31.66%	21.74%	27.28%

Red used for emphasis. SF is Student Fees

To dispel any doubts regarding TWOA achievements, the above data is shown in pie charts. The size of TWOA in 2003 in the selected sector is well demonstrated by the pie charts in Figures 6 and 7. The number of students that TWOA had in 2003, compared with the eight universities, is reflected in the pie chart in Figure 6. Whereas the EFTS that TWOA had in 2003, compared with the eight universities, is reflected in the pie chart in Figure 7.

Figure 6
Student numbers 2003

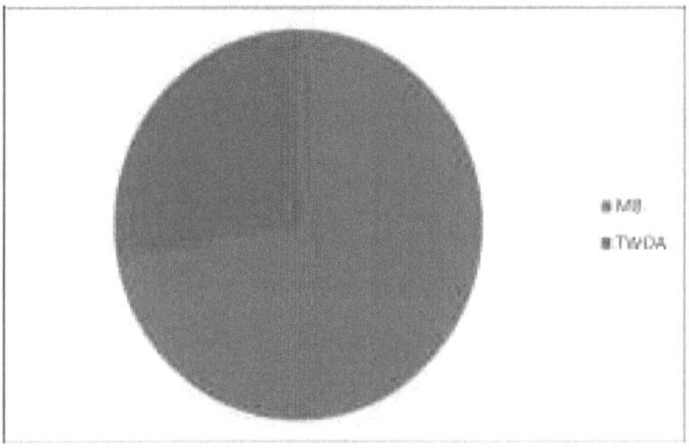

Figure 7
EFTS numbers 2003

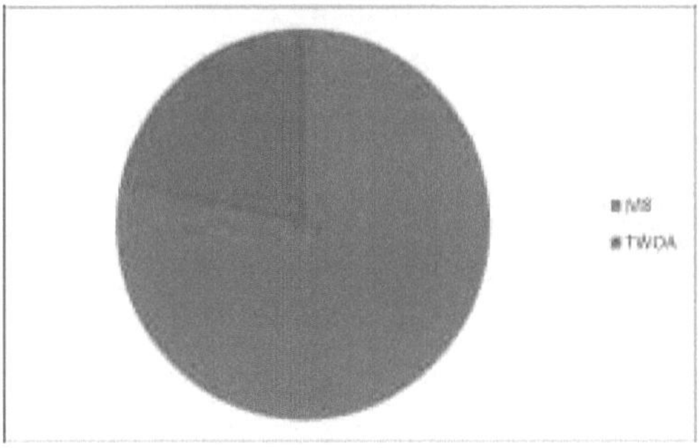

M8 in the above pie charts represents the eight universities; TWOA is just that.

The above is persuasive and compellingly impressive, and shows that TWOA had 'captured' over one quarter (1/4) of the selected sector on every measure.

Clearly, the growth of TWOA would have caught the attention of the funders (the Ministry of Education and the Tertiary Education Commission), and equally, the attention of the eight universities and the Vice Chancellors'

Committee. 2004 saw an unusual amount of labour unrest in the tertiary education sector, with many universities 'crying poor' that they were unable to meet wage demands of staff, threatening staff layoffs due to restrictions on their funding. I believe that this was all rather constructed and closet pressure on the state to do something about the huge amount of funding going to this new boy on the block. It seems to me this was what Dr Ranginui Walker, one time Dean of Māori Studies at the University of Auckland, was talking about when he told me that he was appalled by the actions of his university against TWOA.

On this note, recently, a former Labour Party MP said to me when I was relating this story to him, "Bruce, get real, politicians do nothing unless they are pushed. Think who pushed them?" Well, I have and now I see the significance of Dr Walker's comments.

TWOA massive results were not going un-noticed. The Ministry of Education does periodical reviews of the sector, and in 2003 released their report *Participation in Tertiary Education 2003*. Also in 2003 two independent economic research organisations saw fit to comment on the impact of TWOA from a national economic perspective. Let's have a look at these.

Chapter 6 – What experts said about TWOA

Ministry of Education's observations – (My emphasis in bold type).

Just for the record, the above are verbatim; no embellishment. This is the Ministry's 2003 report. This has to be an A+ by any standard.

Participation in Tertiary Education 2003, states, I quote:

- "Measuring participation is one important indicator of performance of the sector. It measures access to increased learning opportunities, where students hope to take advantage of a range of anticipated benefits. These include the hope of a better job and more income, through to providing life-improving pathways for school leavers, unemployed, or those just seeking to pursue an interest, gain more social interaction, or do something 'useful' with their lives. **There are recognised benefits to society as well from participation in tertiary education, including increased human and social capital, and increased productivity and growth.**
- While growth occurred over most (but not all parts) of the sector, **growth was dominated for the second year running by Te Wānanga o**

Aotearoa. Growth at this provider accounted for 61% of all growth in 2002, making it now the fourth largest provider in terms of headcount at 31st July 2002, and the largest in terms of students enrolled during the year. All Wānanga students numbered over 45,500 in 2002 and these three providers now account for 11% of the sector.

- The rate of participation in 2002 has increased from 19% to 22% for the Māori population aged 15 and over. Even after adjusting for the younger age profile of the Māori population, the **propensity for Māori to engage in tertiary study continues to be higher than for other groups**. However, at degree level Māori participation rates are only 75% of non- Māori rates, while at postgraduate level they are just 60% of non- Māori rates.
- Participation has increased across all levels of study, particularly at certificate and diploma level, where enrolments increased 15% from 2001. Certificate or diploma level is the highest level of study for three in five students (62%). **However, much of the growth at this level is due to the success of Te Wānanga o Aotearoa**. Excluding this provider, certificate level study increased just 4%, and less than the growth at degree and postgraduate levels. Nevertheless, even with this Wānanga excluded, study below

degree level still represents the majority of study (at 58%).

- New Zealand's tertiary education is also currently characterised as being in a period of growth. **The success of the Wānanga (Te Wānanga o Aotearoa, in particular) in attracting first-time Māori students into the sector has seen an explosion in Māori participation at lower levels of the National Qualifications Framework**. Total Māori participation is significantly higher than other groups, even after accounting for the younger age structure of Māori. At degree level and above, however, Māori participation remains lower than non- Māori.
- **Wānanga continued their significant growth** from 2001, increasing by 26,000 students to reach 45,500 in 2002. Wānanga now represent 11% of all students who studied in tertiary institutions in 2002. **The vast majority of these students (94%) were enrolled at Te Wānanga o Aotearoa**. By contrast, the remaining two Wānanga grew by 700 students (29%) and accounted for 2,900 of the 45,500 students attending Wānanga in 2002. **Wānanga students are virtually all domestic**.
- **For a second year, the majority of this growth was in a single provider, Te Wānanga o Aotearoa**. This institution grew from 16,000 students in 2001 to over 42,000 in 2002, an

increase of 26,000 or 168%. Growth at this provider accounted for 61% of all growth in 2002, making it now the fourth largest provider in terms of headcount at 31st July 2002, and the largest in terms of students enrolled during the year. All Wānanga students numbered over 45,500 in 2002 with the three Wānanga now accounting for 11% of the sector.

- **Strong growth continued in the number of Māori** and Asian students, **on the back of significant growth in Wānanga** and international students. Of the 43,000 extra students in 2002, 70% identified with one of these groups. There were 2,500 extra Pasifika students (11% growth) and 20,000 extra Pākehā/Other students (8% growth).
- As in previous years, Māori women are more significantly involved in tertiary than Māori men. 65% of Māori students are women compared with 55% for non- Māori. This holds for all ages, but is more marked at older ages.
- Māori are also more likely to be studying extramurally. Nearly one in three extramural students (33%) was Māori, compared with 17% for intramural students".

NZIER's observations (New Zealand Institute of Economic Research).

Certain extracts of the NZIER 2003 report are specific to the achievements of TWOA.

These are:

- "Many **Te Wānanga courses have no fees** and this appears to have a very significant effect on accessibility. Non-fee courses include Te Ara Reo (Māori language) and Mahi Ora (work skills) courses. **These programmes are cornerstones of the policy to draw people into an environment that is conducive to unblocking impediments to work and further education**.
- An additional plank in the holistic cultural approach is the emphasis placed on **developing international ties with indigenous peoples' institutions.** This has the effect of **broadening out the focus of the institution with the side benefit of adding to New Zealand's international ties**.
- To date, **Te Wānanga has retained its strong focus on 'stair casing' programmes** in employment skills, computing and Te Ara Reo Māori. Its emphasis is on **reducing barriers to entry to these programmes to prospective students in isolated areas in the regions and, importantly, isolated suburbs in metropolitan areas**.
- The emphasis at Te Wānanga has been strongly multi-dimensional in attempting to raise combinations of the cultural, social and material status of students. **Identity and self-esteem are important platforms for personal**

growth in younger tertiary students – they are perhaps even important for 'second chance' students. **Te Wānanga has accordingly emphasized the development of social capital in institutions it uses and the institutional systems it promotes**.

- In relation to the role Te Wānanga played, 'Jane' said she **does not know where she would be now if it weren't for Te Wānanga**. When asked if she could have, or would have, done this course for similar outcomes elsewhere she answered firmly in the negative. She has now overcome the shyness that had played a role in her earlier experiences, as well as enjoying the giving and receiving nature of the feedback loops provided by the teacher/pupil relationship.
- **Wānanga is the largest and arguably one of the most important tertiary institutions in New Zealand**. Its explosive growth over the last five years has **drawn large numbers of people of all ethnic groups mainly into a number of certificate and diploma- level courses**. The vast majority of its students are domestic students, so only relatively few foreign students are enrolled.
- Te Wānanga o Aotearoa students are typically mature people with children, who live in relatively isolated regions, or suburbs. Many have a low income background, and lack the

confidence and/or the formally acquired skills to seriously aspire to the higher earning positions in the modern New Zealand labour market. **They have been engaged into tertiary study and training by Te Wānanga through the use of various innovative strategies** broadly targeted at their groups' specific situation. These initiatives include an active and positive outreach programme that is tailored to the various situations that have been identified.

- Another prominent feature of the Wānanga is the creation of a consciously Māori driven educational institution with a distinctive style; this is built around a deliberate, culturally aware, yet modern, Māori format. While not unique, **its homemade success projects to the students** as a sort of metaphor. It has the virtue of making concrete the idea that unusual and innovative approaches are worthwhile, and can be made to work even by the disadvantaged who are starting from a low base, as long as approached the right way, in today's world).
- There are signs that the very **process of Te Wānanga training and educating is changing people's lives**.
- Looking at the economic value alone, this institution may be seen as having a percentage impact on measurable percentage growth in GDP. On figures cited, rough though these

might be, the **Wānanga's effect on GDP is already approaching the contribution of the forestry sector, or that associated with the foreign students New Zealand takes".**

BERL's observations (Business and Economic Research Limited).

Extracts from this report, which focus on the numbers and make of the student demographics, dated May 2004 are, again, an extract, no embellishment, circumspect, but factual.

- "TWOA has grown in student numbers from around 680 students in 1998 to around 34,000 students in 2003. **This growth rate of almost 5,000% over 5 years or an average annual rate of around 900%.**
- TWOA has a fairly high proportion of female students. In 1998 there was an even split between female and male students where around 51% were male. The **number of women peaked in 2001 at around 74% before falling to around 70%** in 2003.
- **European/Pākehā is now the second largest group at TWOA** accounting for around 19% of all students. This is up from zero in 1998. Similarly Asian students account for around 9% of students, up from one student the year before.
- The main prior activity group for participants at TWOA is wage or salary workers at around 37%

> of all participants. This proportion has stayed the same over the year. **Unemployed/beneficiary is the next largest group at around 30% of all participants"**.

It is very hard to image how anyone, particularly a government that was so passionate and publically committed to increasing participation by the public and Māori particularly into education, could not have been overwhelmed by what Dr Wetere and his team achieved at TWOA. However, as we will find out, behind the scenes, the wolves were circling, looking for a weakness to present itself. Regrettably for them, no weakness appeared. Instead, the wolves created one. Let's see how.

Chapter 7 – Setting the stage

2004 was a definitive year for TWOA. The year started well. TWOA had over $37 million in the bank, and an expectation (based on a legally binding Deed signed by two Cabinet Ministers) of receiving the first instalment of $10 million of a $20 million suspensory loan from the state. It ended with the small window being presented by McNally; the small window that gave dishonourable people a dishonourable weapon.

The Deed of Settlement was, as I said, signed by two Cabinet Ministers on behalf of the Crown, and was the outcome of negotiations between the Crown and TWOA as a result of Waitangi Tribunal recommendations to the Crown. For those of you unfamiliar with the Waitangi Tribunal, it was set up in 1975 for the sole purpose of hearing grievances brought by Māori as a result of past actions of the state against Māori. The Waitangi Tribunal's website states their vision is that, "having reconciled ourselves with the past and possessing a full understanding of the Treaty of Waitangi, Māori and non-Māori New Zealanders will be equipped to create a future for two peoples as one nation".

We know wānanga were created as a result of the Education Amendment Act 1990, the same Act that stated that new TEIs (wānanga) were no longer eligible to receive capital funding from the state. We also know that, up to the passing of this Act, the eight traditional universities in Aotearoa New Zealand had received hundreds of millions of dollars by way of capital from the state.

Wānanga were able to get EFTS funding, calculated by Treasury to provide for the costs of delivery of the course (85%). The balance was for capital maintenance. This model, however, assumes that there is capital to maintain, that is, that the TEI has some capital. Wānanga did not. This led to the conclusion by wānanga collectively that this may have been discriminatory, just the sort of thing that the Waitangi Tribunal was set up to consider.

The case put by wānanga to the Tribunal in 1999 resulted in the Tribunal making recommendations to the state that wānanga should be resourced by the provision of capital funding, so full credit to the Labour government - this is what was done. The outcome for TWOA was a Deed of Settlement signed in November 2001 that gave $40 million to TWOA, with a further $20 million by way of suspensory loan, should EFTS numbers exceed 10,900 by 2003. By 2003 TWOA had achieved 34,500 EFTS, over three times the target figure!

It is important to understand that the amount of $40 million was established as what both parties to the negotiations believed was appropriate at the time of the negotiations, that is up to November 2001. For the 2001 year, TWOA had 6,118 EFTS, therefore, $40 million equates to about $6,500 per EFTS on the basis of the agreed figure in the Deed of Settlement. 10,900 EFTS at the same rate is just over $70 million (an additional $30 million I suggest?) and 34,500 EFTS at the same rate, is $224 million. It is also important to understand that TWOA had no desire or interest to re-visit the figures in the Deed of Settlement. The agreement was made for an additional $20 million, and TWOA was prepared to live with this.

TWOA did not get the $40 million until 2002, in the year that they achieved 20,769 EFTS (nearly twice the target figure for 2003 set in the Deed of Settlement). The whole purpose of this capital funding was to fund capital works, which for a TEI like TWOA, is land, buildings, computers, tables, chairs, infrastructure and the other assets that make a TEI function. As logic would have it, TWOA needed to spend quickly due to the massive number of students coming through their doors, or enrolling in the distance learning programmes. TWOA could not legally accept an enrolment and then fail to provide and deliver to the student, the education services required.

As already stated, TWOA started 2004 with $37 million in the bank, and an expectation of the first instalment of the suspensory loan under the Deed of Settlement signed by two Cabinet Ministers on behalf of the Crown. TWOA was still in growth mode, was blitzing previous student number predictions, and had to provide for its students. TWOA had long run out of motel accommodation in Te Awamutu to accommodate any reasonable numbers of people, and on the recommendation of the Secretary of Education, looked to establishing a central library facility. As Secretary Howard Fancy related to Dr Wetere, a 'real' university needed a library, so that was taken on board by TWOA. You see, TWOA was new to this field, and did not at this stage, have a library.

Like any good business, during budget preparations for 2003, a capital budget had been set for 2004. However because of the massive growth experienced by TWOA, it did not really fit any 'good business' model. Predictions made one year, often were inappropriate when the reality presented itself; just look at the growth rates. In 2004, TWOA decided to buy what was known as the Glenview Hotel. This was a substantial complex as close to Te Awamutu as was possible, and close to the Hamilton airport. The attraction of this site was its size and the fact that it had a large accommodation centre that could be used to overcome the lack of motel space in Te Awamutu, provide accommodation for residential educational courses, and of course, there was room for the central library as proposed by Fancy.

This purchase was a big capital expenditure for TWOA, and had quite extensive refurbishment costs. However, with $37 million in the bank, and another $20 million on the way from the suspensory loan under the Deed of Settlement signed by two Cabinet Ministers on behalf of the Crown, it was viable.

With the benefit of hindsight, had TWOA known the true calibre of the people that they were dealing with at government level, I am sure that TWOA would have exercised a little more restraint. When we examine the process of the suspensory loan later in this narrative, there was no real reason to doubt either the integrity of the process or the people, as the release of the suspensory loan proceeds seemed assured. Again as you will see, even as late as 2nd December 2004, Ministry officials were saying that $5 million would be released prior to Xmas.

Now enter, stage right, another military man, again on the state payroll. Remember Lieutenant-General Sir Cameron in 1863, the one with the state-of-the-art heavy guns? Roll forward the camera to 2005, and let me introduce you to the contributions of one Lieutenant-Colonel Wira Gardiner (Sir, now as well).

Image 13. Sir Harawira 'Wira' Tiri Gardiner: described as 'professional soldier, senior public servant and writer'.

In January or February 2005, he was appointed as a Ministerial appointee to the TWOA Council by Mallard. At his first council meeting in Te Awamutu during February 2005, barely before the karakia was completed, he launched into a tirade of criticism of Dr Wetere, demanding his resignation on the basis that "no competent CEO would spend money before he got it". All the military background, ex Te Puni Kokiri CEO, Government 'fix it man' (I saw somewhere); I suppose gave this gentleman the right to wade straight in, with the delicacy of a loose cannon.

It is inconceivable to me that Sir Wira did not know what the state's agenda was, and that he understood that the state was about to renege on a legal Deed of Settlement to create that small window for some leverage. What staggered me was that TWOA was all about delivering to Sir Wira's people. It was developed by Sir Wira's people for Sir Wira's people, but none of this seemed to matter to Sir Wira in Te Awamutu that day. However, it was very clear to me where the dignity stood. Dr Wetere sat passively, and let Sir Wira have his say. Dr Wetere has a little more to add about Sir Wira at the end of this story.

Despite Sir Wira's criticism, the Dr Wetere did not resign, so on to the next stage.

Chapter 8. The hysteria

The stage was set. McNally had pointed the Minister of Education to the small window and Sir Wira had done his best to rough up Dr Wetere. This did not faze Dr Wetere. Therefore, plan B for the state.

On 15th February 2005, the Honourable Ken Shirley MP, at the time, deputy leader of the ACT Party, said in the House of Parliament, under parliamentary privilege, that he was in possession of 'leaked' information. He stated:

> "I think the House and the country at large is (sic) concerned at the lack of accountability that has been exposed in Te Wānanga o Aotearoa. The Government's representative on the governing board, Mr. McNally, has described a culture of executive extravagance. Yet we have also learnt this week that, under this Labour Government, funding for the wānanga went from $8 million per year to $239 million last year. That is over a quarter of a billion dollars of taxpayers' money".

Further:

> "Let us have a look at some of the governance issues. It is clear that a group of people in this organisation are getting very, very rich, at the taxpayers' expense. When we look at the governance situation there are a number of issues. The key question is: why has the Government not

> moved to address these problems? One thing we do know is that one of the major programmes, the Mahi Ora programme, was developed by a staff member and sold to the wānanga for $7 million. That was $7 million of taxpayers' money".
>
> "There are dozens of these shelf companies. If we look at the ownership structure of these companies—the shareholders and the directors—they are all cross-pollinated. It would seem that all the same people are cross-pollinating these companies, clipping the taxpayers' ticket, and rorting the taxpayers of this country".

Further:

> "In light of the fact that the cap imposed by this Government saw the funding expand from $8 million to $239 million, can the Minister tell us what is his response to the fact that Te Wānanga o Aotearoa runs a corporate fleet of over 350 staff cars, including LTD limos".

The Honourable Ken Shirley is an interesting person. He first entered parliament in the 1984 elections as a Labour Party member; aligning himself with Roger Douglas, and became a notable supporter of the reforms that Douglas promoted. Shirley briefly held Cabinet rank as Minister of Fisheries, Associate Minister of Agriculture, Associate Minister of Forestry, and Associate Minister of Health. He lost these positions when the Labour Party was defeated in the 1990 elections and he also lost his Tasman seat, leaving him outside parliament.

After being sacked from Labour, Douglas created the ACT New Zealand Party. Shirley, now a member of ACT, was involved their first campaign in the 1996 elections, he was ranked in third place on the ACT Party list; and re-entered parliament as a list MP in that year. He has served as ACT's deputy leader, and in 2004, he was one of four candidates to seek the party's leadership, but he failed with this. He sought election as Speaker of the House of Representatives, but was placed third. He remained a list MP until the 2005 election, in which only two ACT MPs were returned. He is now out of parliament.

Image 14. Ken Shirley.

Ken Shirley is what is known in Aotearoa New Zealand as a waka jumper. However, that did not mean that he no longer had a use to Labour. I wonder where his 'leaked' information came from. Not too much of a leap of a faith to solve that one is there? Shirley made some very serious allegations under parliamentary privilege, but predictably did not have the evidence and I suggest, the courage or conviction, to make these allegations outside the house, as he was were invited to by Dr Wetere.

It is time to put Ken Shirley's statements under the spotlight, as I think that the public should know what it was, as Mallard's mouthpiece, he had to say behind the curtain of parliamentary privilege. Shirley's comments are in quotes. My replies are in bold type.

- "Massive level of funding of $239 million in 1 year". **The most TWOA ever received in a year was $178 million. Sure this was a heap of money but why increase it by nearly $60 million?**
- "McNally advised in December of a serious breakdown in financial management, with a prevailing culture of non-accountability and extravagance in wānanga spending by senior management". **If so, whom did he advise and how? Certainly not the Council of TWOA, and despite a complete review of all records from the Ministry of Education under the Official Information Act, I have found nothing along these lines.**
- "It is clear that a group of people in this organisation are getting very, very rich, at the taxpayers' expense". **There are accusations**

of dodgy, even illegal acts in this statement. But no details of who, how and when. I know who got what, and who got nothing. I know who worked for several years at rates that the Ken Shirley's would never have worked for. I have the evidence, and also isn't it funny that the Auditor General, the NZ Police, or Serious Fraud Office, did not pick up on anyone getting "very, very rich"?

- "One thing we do know is that one of the major programmes, the Mahi Ora programme, was developed by a staff member and sold to the wānanga for $7 million. That was $7 million of taxpayers' money". **Essentially correct.** **But it was not a staff member and sure as heck not the CEO's fiancé as you later suggested. It is a matter of public record who was paid $7 million, and it is a matter of public record that three independent valuations from the likes of KPMG were received before this deal was done. It also is a matter of public record that Dr Wetere exercised the very best of governance practices by totally excluding himself from all discussions relating to the decisions for this purchase. The purchase subsequently provided over $100 million in revenues to TWOA, all earned under the policies of the time.**

➢ "There are dozens of these shelf companies. If we look at the ownership structure of these companies—the shareholders and the directors—they are all cross-pollinated. It would seem that all the same people are cross-pollinating these companies, clipping the taxpayers' ticket, and rorting the taxpayers of this country". **Ken Shirley shows his ignorance here. Shelf companies are just that. They are not trading. They don't have any money. There are no tickets to clip. There was however two trading companies associated with TWOA. One was MO1 Limited, which ran the Mahi Ora programme. Because of the big bucks used to buy this programme, the governing body of TWOA thought it was justified to micro managing it. Not a new idea, simply practical good sense, but then again can practical, good sense, be expected from a Māori organization? The other entity was Oma Investments Limited. Not even owned by TWOA but by Aotearoa Institute. This was set up to purchase resources for TWOA that could not be purchased at reasonable cost in Aotearoa New Zealand. For instances, Canterbury Clothing thought all of their birthdays had come at once when TWOA asked them to supply 25,000 jackets for their students. From memory they quoted $190 each.**

TWOA therefore decided to do what the Warehouse does. They looked to China. If my memory serves me correct again, Oma Investments paid $35 each for these from China. There was a technical problem though. Should or can a TEI get involved in purchasing overseas and be exposed to the resulting exchange risks? TWOA did not think so, so therefore AI came to the party. Aotearoa Institute made $3 million from importing resources for TWOA, and rebated the full amount back to TWOA. It is a charitable trust after all and that is what these things do. Again a matter of public record.

- "The fact that Te Wānanga o Aotearoa runs a corporate fleet of over 350 staff cars, including LTD limos". **Corporate? No. TWOA is a TEI, but that is not the point. TWOA has never owned one LTD 'limo'. The LTD 'limo' driven by the Tumuaki was and is still owned by AI. This arrangement worked from the beginning and no one really cared about asking TWOA to buy it. A fleet of cars? Sure thing, horses, and donkeys might be more appropriate for a Māori organization in some people's mind, but the facts are; TWOA had over 25,000 students on the Mahi Ora distance learning programme, which is just that, they do not have to come to a campus.**

> **The reason that so many people did not come to the campuses of the eight mainstream universities, was because they couldn't get to the campuses. Like: no car, push bike, donkey, horse, or the thing that makes bus trips possible: money. TWOA was dealing with under-privileged people who wished to change their place in life for themselves and their children. TWOA took the mountain to Mohammed, they took the kaitiaki (guardian) to the students, out in the back of beyond, where Telecom had in many cases, long since cut the phone off, and where buses didn't always run.**

A little fact finding before Shirley fronted for Mallard, would certainly have earned him my respect, but for those few moments in the spotlight, his objectivity was just blinded, and he showed us what sort of a person he really is.

The following day, on 16th February 2005 (and reported almost daily from that date), a NZ Herald article was headed, "Wānanga chief pledges to open books to any inquiry" included statements such as "nothing less than a disaster"; and a "culture of non-accountability and extravagance"; with the next day's edition referring to "a series of rorts by wānanga bosses through connections between them and outside companies", and "a course was sold to the Te Wānanga o Aotearoa for an extraordinary seven-figure sum by the chief executive's fiancé". And there was the old one, but a good one: nepotism at TWOA.

You must understand that we are talking about an initiative that started in Te Awamutu, a small rural town, probably as far from the coast as most places in Aotearoa New Zealand. The population at the time was about 10,000, no university, no live theatre, and not many real corporate opportunities for the upwardly mobile. The reality is that most businesses in Te Awamutu have at sometime employed a spouse, brother or sister, or one of the children (read whānau). Just about all of my school friends from farms, went to work on their Dad and Mum's farm at one time or other.

Attracting any staff to a small Māori Private Training Enterprise, which then became a small TEI, from outside of the local area, was just not an attractive career choice. Apart from that, until about 2002, the funds just were not available to pay anything like decent, competitive salaries. Levelling charges of nepotism as Ken Shirley did against TWOA, is and was gross ignorance. However, the public brought it, so why let a few facts get in the way of a good story?

These were the first of a barrage of attacks against Dr Wetere and TWOA. An examination of New Zealand Parliamentary Debates records, Hansards, over the following months shows many damaging and derogatory statements directed towards Dr Wetere, TWOA and its staff. There was a great emphasis, with clear insinuations, that Dr Wetere was employing some of his family (whānau) alongside him, with "many people getting very rich". The clear purpose of these attacks, in my opinion, was the state preparing the public for what they intended to do, that is, to neutralise Dr Wetere, and to then take control of TWOA. The fact that the allegations were completely without foundations, as we will find out, was of no concern to the protagonists.

It is interesting to wind back to 1863; there are some fine comparisons here. More déjà vu? In preparation for the 'invasion' of the Waikato, the press of the day, no doubt fed by the politicians, wrote of the rebellious savages who were planning to invade Auckland, and cause all kind of mayhem for the settlers. By way of example, look at the rhetoric in the preamble to the New Zealand Settlement Act 1863 (my bold type for emphasis):

> "Whereas the Northern Island of the Colony of New Zealand has from time to time been subject to insurrections amongst the **evil disposed persons of the Native race to the great alarm and intimidation of Her Majesty's peaceful subjects** of both races and involving great losses of life and expenditure of money in their suppression, and whereby **many outrages** upon lives and property have recently been **committed and such outrages are still threatened and of almost daily occurrence**, and whereas a large number of inhabitants of several districts of the Colony have entered into combinations and **taken up arms** with the object of **attempting the extermination or expulsion of the European settlers**

and are now engaged in **open rebellion against Her Majesty's authority"**.

These "evil disposed persons of the Native race" were of course Māori trying to protect their lands, themselves, their women and children from being invaded by a foreign power with very big guns; a situation that I can understand, one would get quite passionate about. Maybe we have progressed slightly as the cannons were not brought out in 2005, but as we all know, the pen is often cited as being more powerful than the sword.

So we had the first round with the attempted Sir Wira rough up of Dr Wetere; and the second with the public being softened up by Shirley with his florid and extreme accusations, and what always seem to work in Aotearoa New Zealand; Māori bashing, as demonstrated so well by another politician, Don Brash.

Image 15. Donald "Don" Thomas Brash (born 1940), 'a New Zealand politician, was Leader of the Opposition, parliamentary leader of the National Party from 28 October 2003 to 27 November 2006 and then the leader of the ACT Party for 28 April 2011 - 26 November 2011'.

Brash was one time leader of the National Party (yes, it is confusing, isn't it). That party was smashed to pieces in the 2002 general election, and the party was toast. A speech by Brash, by then leader of the National Party, in Owera in January 2004 aimed at the privileges 'enjoyed' by Māori (I cringe to write this), and the next day, Brash and his party's toast, was dripping with honey. As a result, he nearly led his party to an election win in the 2006 election. Another waka jumper our Don; he reappeared again in the 2011 election as leader of the ACT Party, the same party that Shirley jumped to.

Chapter 9 - The state's actions

I believe that the public had been deluded into believing that a Māori organisation was at it again. The indignation that followed on talk back radio; the "I told you so" from the rednecks, was deafening. It was therefore now time for a firm hand from those who should be obeyed; that is, those that make up the state.

The first substantive justification that the state gave for their actions against TWOA was in the Aide memoire by Mallard to Cabinet of 28th February 2005, a mere 13 days after the Shirley outbursts. This document set out the state's position and intentions in respect of TWOA, with Mallard justifying his proposed actions by a series of issues he noted in the memoire, which I shall shortly address.

The second substantive justification was contained in Mallard's letter to the TWOA Council on 20th June 2005. This was well after Mallard had control of TWOA's cheque book and had his man Roache, in control of the finances, as he said he would in the Aide memoire. However, the problem for Mallard was that Dr Wetere had not, by 20 June 2005, resigned.

The Aide memoire was notification by Mallard to his Cabinet that he was to appoint a Crown observer to TWOA, who shortly thereafter became the Crown Manager. This appointment effectively put the financial control of TWOA, in the hands of the state. The 20th June 2005 letter was Mallard giving notice that he was considering dissolving the

TWOA Council and appointing a Commissioner in its place. The appointment of a Commissioner would certainly have led to Dr Wetere being dismissed from his position at TWOA. Again, he gave his justifications for this proposed action. Both of these documents initiated by Mallard need to be critically considered to allow you to judge whether Mallard and his team, stretched the truth and used misinformation to achieve their objective, which it becomes very clear, was to pressure Dr Wetere into resigning.

There are five key aspects of the Aide memoire that need examining to test their validity, appropriateness and Mallard's reasoning. Remember, that for his plans and proposition to have any substance under the Education Amendment Act 1990, he had to attempt to put TWOA into a position where it might be in breach of certain sections of that Act, and as you will see, reneging on the terms of the Deed of Settlement in respect of the suspensory loan, which was well overdue for payment by 28th February 2005, was a key part of his game plan. Clearly, Mallard was starting to use the leverage that McNally so eloquently referred to in his 17th December 2004 email.

Mallard states in paragraph 4 of the Aide memoire:

> "That as the wānanga have not met the conditions to access the suspensory loan, I will not be recommending to Cabinet that the wānanga be given access to the suspensory loan at this time".

He then went on to justifying his decision, with the following key aspects:

1. Access to suspensory loan by TWOA

The first key aspect of the justification used by Mallard to deny TWOA the suspensory loan was the "achievement by established criteria".

Mallard states in the third paragraph of the Aide memoire that there was "no report on achievement". The Ministry of Education paper *Participation in Tertiary Education 2003*, discussed on page 64, certainly is very complimentary regarding TWOA's achievements, but if Mallard is referring here to Māori student numbers, then he is totally incorrect. Student profiles, which include the percentage of Māori students enrolled, are published in each of the Annual Reports for TWOA, as is required by the Education Act 1990. It may have been that Mallard meant there were no established criteria on enrolments agreed upon by the parties.

According to evidence presented to the Waitangi Tribunal, (Wai.1298) Frecklington a senior manager at TAMU was of the opinion that Mallard had no right to deny access to the suspensory loan on the grounds of "material achievements". On 9th June 2005, Frecklington said that the only measure not reached was student profiles, which was a delicate issue that Crown Law advice stipulated was not to be imposed on a TEI. This is demonstrated by his advice to Hipkins, senior adviser to Mallard, when he stated ('his abbreviations'):

> "To be absolutely clear, none of the payments made under the Settlement Deed were mistakes. They were made in accordance with the Deed of

> 's/ment'.
>
> It was up to the 'Secty' (of Education) to determine whether material achievement had been reached. He could not deny payment solely because of one measure not being reached.
>
> Some measures were more significant than others. The most 'impt' were student numbers – student profiles and educational outcomes. The only one of these that was not met was student profile, which is the one that required 80% of students to be Māori. This was a delicate issue, and we had Crown Law advice that this stipulation was not legal to be imposed on a TEI. Therefore, no payments were withheld simply because of the percentage of Māori students".

Mallard knew this quota question to be discriminatory, as is indicated in his reply to a question asked of him in Parliament on 9th June 2005, regarding why payments were made to TWOA under the Deed of Settlement in 2002 and 2003 (the $15 million) when the 80% figure for Māori participation was not met. Mallard was asked the following question:

> "Has the Minister seen official advice tendered to him on 23rd December 2004 that stated that the additional redress of $15 million was payable only on condition of certain performance measures, as indicated in the deed, being met; and as it now appears that the payments were made in 2002 and 2003 without performance measures having been

> met, why did he pay millions of dollars to the wānanga when it had not met the conditions for the payment".

Mallard replied:

> "The matter was subject to Crown Law advice around whether conditions had been met. The specific condition that I am advised was not met was in relation to the enrolment of students who were Māori. There was a requirement to have a minimum of 6,400 students who were Māori, as part of the Deed of Settlement requirements. The wānanga actually had 20,400 students who were Māori. With the proportions set out in the Deed of Settlement, there was a maximum of 6,800 Pākehā students. Unfortunately, there was a breach in that the wānanga had nearly 14,000 Pākehā students. I think that to withhold a payment—and, certainly, this is the advice that I have now received, confirmed by Crown Law—because too many white people were enrolled, would have been unreasonable".

The payments referred to were the additional redress amounts made in 2002 and 2003 under the same Deed of Settlement that provided for the payment of the suspensory loan. The additional redress payments and the suspensory loan had identical material achievement criteria, such as student profiles and educational outcomes. This certainly is different from the view he stated in his Aide memoire of 28th February 2005 to Cabinet.

In that memoire, Mallard stated that a key reason for denying TWOA access to the suspensory loan was the percentage of Māori students enrolled at TWOA. Yet he acknowledged in June 2005, that Crown Law had advised him at least as early as December 2004, that it was illegal to deny payment of the suspensory loan on the basis of the percentage of Māori students. If he did not know that in February 2005, he should have. It appears to me that Mallard knew this in 2002, and therefore the achievement by established criteria could not be justification to deny TWOA the proceeds of the suspensory loan to TWOA.

2. Agreement regarding conversion of the suspensory loan to equity.

The second key issue of Mallard's justification not to pay the suspensory loan is in paragraph four of the Aide memoire and related to future key performance indicators (KPIs) for conversion of the loan to equity (rather than repay) that had not been agreed on between the Secretary for Education and TWOA.

As we go through the progress of the negotiations between the state's representatives and members of TWOA in detail in Chapter 11, I believe that you will conclude that there seemed to be goodwill at a high level within the Ministry of Education to resolve issues regarding an agreement on criteria for the release of the suspensory loan to TWOA. We will see that two Draft Agreements were presented in December 2004, which were designed to address the KPI matters. Associated correspondence will show that there was very close agreement between the negotiating parties, until late in December 2004, that is, before McNally's 17th December 2004 email that alerted the Ministry to the small window.

You will also see that little attention seems to have been given by either party to what the KPIs would be for the conversion of the suspensory loan to equity. It may have been that this was not a highly important issue to TWOA, because if agreement could not be reached on the conversion factors, then TWOA simply would have repaid the loan.

3. Crown Observer appointment.

The third key issue raised by Mallard was his intentions to appoint a Crown Observer. His Aide memoire stated that he would use the provisions of section 195C of the Education Act 1989 to do so, which states:

> "A Minister may appoint Crown observer:
>
> (1) If the Minister considers on reasonable grounds that the operation or long-term viability of an institution is at risk, he or she may appoint a Crown observer to the Council of the institution.
>
> (2) A Crown observer may not be appointed to the Council of an institution unless the Minister has first—
>
> (a) Consulted with the Council; and

(b) Advised the Council that he or she is considering appointing a Crown observer; and

(c) Given the Council an opportunity to comment on the proposal.

(3) Every appointment under this section must be in writing and must state the date on which it takes effect.

(4) A Crown observer may—

(a) Attend any meeting of the Council or committee of the Council of the institution to which he or she is appointed; and

(b) Offer advice to the Council, or any committee or member of the Council; and

(c) Report to the Minister on any matter raised or discussed at any meeting that he or she attends as a Crown observer.

(5) A Crown observer must at all times maintain confidentiality with respect to Council affairs, except as authorised by paragraph (c) of subsection (4).

(6) A Crown observer is not a member of the Council or any committee of the Council, and may not—

a) Vote on any matter; or

> b) Exercise any of the powers, or perform any of the functions or duties, of a member of the Council".

The Aide memoire went on to state that the Crown Observer will by the end of March:

> "a) Advise whether there are appropriate, achievable financial plans in place for 2005;
>
> b) On the basis of those plans and other information, advise whether the proposed Crown loan will be used appropriately to support the wānanga's core education function. In this regard I will want assurances that it will not be used for payments to third parties other than as needed for core functions and is not simply to be used to offset poor or unjustifiably weak financial performance; and
>
> c) Advise whether the institution is likely to face serious financial issues in 2005".

In respect of a), this does not appear to be covered by the criteria set out in section 195C of the Education Act 1989, unless this is covered by paragraph (c) of subsection (4). In respect of b) this does not appear to be covered by the criteria set out in section 195C of the Education Act 1989. This may be covered by paragraph (c) of subsection (4), but it does not appear that the dispersal of funds by a TEI for legitimate purposes is a justification for the use of the provisions of 195C. This is an issue that is at the core of the independence provisions for TEIs, and was promoted as one of the foundation principles of the Education Amendment Act 1990. Mere detail?

In respect of c), it appears that section 195C gives the Minister the power to appoint a Crown Observer only if, on reasonable grounds, he considers that the operation or long-term viability of a TEI is at risk. Section 195C does not provide the power to appoint a Crown Observer to **see** whether an institution is at risk.

To the crux of this matter however, is why would Mallard need all of this rhetoric when he already had McNally doing his beckoning as is evidenced by the McNally emails? Those emails to Mallard's Ministry on 17th and 21st December 2004 show that Mallard already had what he envisaged by invoking sec 195C, in Graeme McNally, albeit under the disguise of Development Advisor. Whether or not McNally was in breach of his fiduciary obligations to TWOA Council by these emails, is a debate for another day. In my opinion, he definitely was.

4. Proper use of funds

The fourth key issue identified by Mallard was relating to him having confidence that "funds will be properly accounted for". The Public Finance Act, along with the International Financial Reporting Standards and the Crimes Act in Aotearoa New Zealand, apart from the rigours of statutory required annual audits, generally ensure that "funds are properly accounted for".

I believe Mallard was referring to what was reported in the NZ Herald on 25th February 2005:

> "Sources say Dr Wetere approached Finance Minister Michael Cullen last year about accessing the suspensory loan facility and wanted to use the bulk of it to repay one of its subsidiary trusts for intellectual and capital property it had invested in the wānanga.
>
> Critics claim this would be an abuse of taxpayers' money and say it is one reason the Government is wary of approving the loan, which would not have to be paid back. Chen Palmer has confirmed the wānanga had instructed it to advice on whether the settlement reached with the Crown was being honoured. Accounting firm Ernst and Young is understood to have advised the wānanga council its proposal was viable".

TWOA's position in respect of this likely claim, was made clear by TWOA in their audited financial statements for the year ended 31st December 2003 noted (p. 118) under the heading of Contingencies in the Statement of Commitments and Contingencies was:

> "Aotearoa Institute Charitable Trust has indicated that it intends making a claim against Te Wānanga o Aotearoa for intellectual property and artworks transferred to Te Wānanga o Aotearoa on its formation. At present, the amount or eventual outcome of the claim is unknown and no provision has been made in the financial statements".

The situation regarding this transaction was the subject of a letter from the Chair of TWOA (Coxhead) to Mallard and Maharey on 25th November 2004, and states that the matter was brought to the attention of the Tertiary Advisory & Monitoring Unit (TAMU – Sargison's outfit!) in letters of 20th July 2004, 15th September 2004 and 3rd November 2004. These letters confirmed that TWOA and AI had jointly funded the reports from lawyers, Bell Gully and accountants Ernst and Young, with the Chair of Ernst and Young (who was also the New Zealand Round Table Chair at the time), nominated to lead the review and valuation.

The Coxhead letter reported that Bell Gully and Ernst and Young had recommended a midpoint valuation $12.3 million to compensate AI for the use of its intellectual property up until the date of their report, with an ongoing annual compensation amount paid by TWOA to AI, calculated at 10.2% of Te Ara Reo Māori course revenues.

To reiterate what Mallard said:

> "The wānanga has increased pressure on the Crown to make this loan and retained Chen and Palmer to assist. I have made it clear that there can be no question of the loan proceeding until due process has been completed, the case established and the Crown given confidence that the funds will be property used".

It would appear that Mallard was not impressed with the idea that firms with the reputations of Bell Gully, Chen Palmer and Ernst and Young were involved, and also unimpressed with the thought that Aotearoa Institute may be reimbursed for what it had made available to TWOA. The fact that the Coxhead letter indicated clear agreement between TWOA and AI to resolve this issue seems to have caused Mallard some concern. However, this all misses the point though, as what a TEI does with its money is an issue for the TEI Council and not a matter for a Minister of Education, under the independence provisions of the Education Amendment Act 1990.

5. Short term funding

Mallard stated in his Aide memoire that short term financial cash flow issues of TWOA could and should be dealt with through overdraft facilities. A great and incisive observation by Mallard, but while this may have been correct in 'normal' circumstances, it certainly was not the case in February 2005 for TWOA, after the huge amount of adverse publicity that it had received in that month, thanks to Shirley.

The facts regarding the availability of overdraft facilities for TWOA after the February assaults by the state are shown in documents obtained by Chen Palmer from an examination of the Ministry of Education files. A document "TWOA application for Crown Loan" from the Crown Manager (PWC Roache, whom we are yet to meet) stated "that the potential to arrange a borrowing facility with a commercial bank to meet the short term requirements has been considered [with BNZ]. The impact of the bad publicity that TWOA suffered in February 2005 had the following results:

- It was apparent from the discussion that:
    - Any application would receive very close scrutiny from the banks credit committee and they would be particularly cautious about advancing credit;
    - They were generally nervous about the negative publicity surrounding the institution".

This is the old trick. Cut off the suspensory loan proceeds of a Deed signed by two Cabinet Ministers, and then cut off the supply of credit by scaring the daylights out of the banks. Talk about a siege mentality! Colonialism 101 in full flight!

Just to reiterate. A summary of the key issues raised by Mallard as justification for his action were – my responses in bold:

- Access to suspensory loan. **As reported by the Minister of Education to Parliament, the use of this student profile criterion was illegal. Whether Mallard knew this or not in February 2005 is unclear, but a precedent had been created with the payment of the $15 million 'additional redress' in 2002 and 2003, when the percentage of Māori students was below the Deed of Settlement benchmark of 80%.**
- Agreement regarding conversion of suspensory loan. **It would appear that there was no willingness for the state to do this after the "just a small window for some leverage" email.**

The Crown loan (which really was the suspensory loan in drag, as you will see) that took the place of the suspensory loan, was advanced in May 2005, and was certainly repaid in full by TWOA by 31st December 2007, and enabled conditions that were not part of the suspensory loan agreement to be attached to the Crown loan.

- Crown Observer appointment. **Mallard already had many of the powers that Section 195C envisaged, provides to him by way of the Development Advisor (McNally). The reasons given by Mallard for the appointment of a Crown Observer appear to be outside of the scope of Section195C of the Education Act 1989. Maybe he was the exercising ministerial discretion?**
- Proper use of funds. **This justification appears to relate to the proposed transaction that had been agreed to by the Council of TWOA and the Board of AI. A Minister's involvement in an issue of this nature are in my view, outside of a Minister's powers in respect of TEI's as made plain by the Education Amendment Act 1990.**
- Short term funding. **The importance of the proceeds of the suspensory loan for the 'financial health' of TWOA was apparent to Dr Wetere as early as September 2004, when he signalled to Mallard that capital expenditure**

> **had been accelerated to provide for the growth that TWOA was experiencing. The Finance Director of TWOA in December 2004 also signalled this to the TWOA Council, the Ministry, and the Development Advisor in December 2004.**

In fact, apart from a large amount of negative publicity about TWOA generated by Mallard in February 2005, very little was put forward by him to justify the appointment of the Crown Observer who then became Crown Manager. Everyone at TWOA knew that McNally was a defacto Crown Observer, as he demonstrated by his December 2004 emails to the Ministry. If there was a pending financial crisis at TWOA, it was Mallard's creation, created by using the leverage that McNally pointed him to.

The Aide memoire was justification for denying TWOA the proceeds of the suspensory loan, and for the appointment of a man who became the Crown Manager. This man was Brian Roache, a partner at the time, of PriceWaterhouseCooper. Of course the TWOA Council by this time had to make this appointment, but believe me, these Councillors had become a little shell shocked by this stage. They had collectively put up with a huge barrage from the media, and all kinds of official letters with foreign names, and I guess that the consensus at the time was if a Crown Manager got the suspensory loan money that was deservedly and legally due to TWOA, then what the heck.

Enter Roache of PWC (now ex PWC); another interesting person. One of those who seem to pop up with similar regularity as Sir Wira, McNally, and Sargison do in the Government appointed positions. Roache and his team from PWC arrived fully power suited, and with all the current corporate speech flowing, in Te Awamutu in early March 2005. They were evangelical in their approach to righting the wrongs that they had been briefed about. Well I think they were; but I guess at a fee of $90,000 per month for what was to be for over three years, payable by TWOA, you would give one a slightly elevated view on life. Predictably, they took control of the cheque book. Game one to the state!

Just to recount; the state had the cheque book out of TWOA's hands, and Roache was in full control of all of the financial affairs of TWOA.

Image 16. Brian Roache: ex PWC partner, now CEO of NZ Post.

One would have thought that Mallard would have been pretty happy about this. However, the problem was that Dr Wetere was still in place and TWOA's parent entity AI, in funds and actively preparing a visit to the Waitangi Tribunal. The state's objective of removing Dr Wetere had failed. Therefore Plan B was called for. This was Mallard's letter of the 20th July 2005 to TWOA.

This document also needs scrutiny, as I believe that it is clear that the Aide memoire was based on some very doubtful grounds. Mallard's July letter expressed the "preliminary view that the Council should be dissolved and a Commissioner appointed in its place". As this letter was written several months after the Crown Manager had taken control of the finances of TWOA, and a Crown loan advanced, this view could not have been formed as a consequence of financial issues.

The document provides justification for the actions that Mallard was contemplating, in terms of the risk criteria published in the NZ Gazette under section 195A of the Education Act 1989, specifically. In my view, its only purpose could have been to shock the TWOA Council into delivering Dr Wetere's head to Mallard.

The key points were:

Criterion 22. The time period, (4 months) for submitting the 2004 audited financial statements had expired.

Criterion 25. That TWOA approved an unauthorised loan to Aotearoa Institute.

Criterion 33. There is no business plan for 2004 and 2005 financial years.

Criterion 34. Changes by government to funding priorities will likely expose the Institution to a material reduction of income.

Criterion 35. From May onwards, the cash flow indicated that (without assistance from the Crown in the form of a short term advance of $12 million on 16th May 2005) the institution is not likely to pay some or all of its debts as they become due in the ordinary course of business.

Mallard adds, "Of these, I wish to make it clear that it is the viability of the institution as a going concern that I consider to be the main serious risk".

To reiterate, the facts at this stage were that Mallard's man Roache controlled the TWOA cheque book and finances; Mallard controlled the release of the suspensory loan funding, and he controlled the EFTS funding that TWOA was generating. So why should he claim that going concern was the main serious risk? From an accounting point of view, it is only ever with the benefit of hindsight that one can be sure of that an entity can pass the going concern test.

We now have that hindsight: TWOA is still alive and kicking strong, albeit more in Mallard's mould and only one third of its previous size. Was it ever in risk of failing the going concern test? There was only person on this earth that could have put TWOA in that position in June 2005; Mallard.

Let us now look at what he put forward to bully the Council into sending Dr Wetere packing, as the appointment of a Commissioner would surely have resulted in.

Mallard's criterion and my responses:

Criterion 22 – Audit Report in 4 months from balance date.

The auditors of TWOA for several years were Deloitte, (McNally's firm) appointed to act as agents of the Auditor General of New Zealand. I believe that they had carried out the audit for at least three years up to 2004, and I know they audited the financial statements for the year ended 31st December 2007. I conclude that as a result of their several years' involvement, they had a full understanding of the TWOA and its principal executives, because up to 31st December 2003 they had only issued what was then referred to as unqualified Audit Reports. An unqualified Audit Report? That means all is honky dory and Deloitte remember, on behalf of the Auditor General – are up there with the best, if not the best!

On 15th February 2005, six weeks after TWOA's balance date, Shirley started his rantings in Parliament regarding the affairs of TWOA. I don't think that we need to honour these utterances by mentioning them again, but you will also not be surprised they were followed shortly by the Prime Minister saying that the Controller and Auditor General (OAG) would be carrying out an investigation into the affairs of TWOA.

What must be understood, and I am sure that Mallard knew this, that if an auditor reads the types of statements about an organisation that he/she is auditing, such as those said by Shirley under parliamentary privilege, it tends to raise serious risk issues and concerns for the auditor. Therefore, having had all of the allegations voiced in public as Mallard did, made it totally unreasonable to expect the auditors of TWOA (or in fact any organisation) could or would have complete their audit of the financial statements of TWOA for the year ended 31st December 2004, within four months of balance date.

The Controller and Auditor General, in his report '*Inquiry into certain aspects of Te Wānanga o Aotearoa*', date 1st December 2005, stated:

> "We began an audit and inquiry into Te Wānanga o Aotearoa (TWOA) after receiving a request for assurance from the then Associate Minister of Education (Tertiary Education) in September 2004. There were concerns about possible conflicts of interest in transactions worth large sums of money. Other issues emerged as we began our inquiry".

It is noteworthy that the TWOA Council was not aware that the Auditor General had any serious interest in TWOA in September 2004. I am sure if they had, this would have been brought to the Council, directly by the Auditor General.

The OAG further stated:

> "In February 2005, then MP the Honourable Ken Shirley and the media made certain allegations. The then Minister of Education asked us to look into more matters. We reconsidered the scope of our work, released wider terms in March 2005, and

continued with our inquiry".

With all of this in the public domain, it is no surprise that the audit for the year ended 31st December 2004 was not completed until 31st August 2007 by Deloitte, on behalf of the Auditor-General. It did miss the 4 month time period by a little, by 27 months in fact, but this was the obvious outcome since Shirley let loose under parliamentary privilege.

Criterion 25 – AI loan

In this Criterion Mallard refers to a conveniently termed "unauthorised" loan to AI by TWOA. As has been discussed earlier, by 1993 AI had accumulated several buildings from which it had been carrying out its activities as an educational provider prior to the formation of TWOA. In addition to land and buildings, AI accumulated the normal chattels of an educational provider, such as vehicles, teaching resources, staff, intellectual property, infrastructure, and extensive artworks, which were made available to TWOA by AI, at zero consideration.

We know that six years after being granted TEI status, wānanga collectively lodged a claim with the Waitangi Tribunal for capital funding, and we know that TWOA entered into two Deeds of Settlement, in December 2000 and November 2001 with the Crown. The funds released by these Deeds were used to increase resources for the TWOA students, not to purchase any assets of AI. In fact, at no time up to the date of the state onslaught, TWOA had not paid one cent to AI, apart from rather belated rental payments for the lease of various AI premises.

During the 2001 financial year, prior to the November 2001 settlement agreement, TWOA Council decided that a prominent presence in the Wellington region was important. They recognised that there was a potentially large student target group in the Porirua region, an area with high unemployment and a population largely made up of Māori and Pacific Island people. What was then known as the Todd building was available for purchase at approximately $12 million. This building was considered ideal, and an agreement for sale and purchase was entered into.

At this stage, AI had a considerable asset base resulting from the pre - 1993 land and building purchases, and TWOA, without state provided capital, had little. AI also had a borrowing capability that TWOA lacked. The purchase was therefore settled in the name of the AI who provided $9 million, and AI then borrowed $3 million from TWOA. It must be noted that this purchase was settled before the Deed of Settlement of 6th November 2001, that released $40 million to TWOA during 2002, was completed. Apart from EFTS funding, which is constructed to principally cover operational and delivery costs, TWOA did not have the funds to affect this purchase in its own right, and used the $40 million for many other capital requirements needed to resource TWOA students.

TWOA was concerned about the prudence of lending funds to AI, albeit that AI was the founding entity, so the Chair of TWOA rang the Secretary for Education (Howard Fancy) for his approval, which was given. It appears that

Fancy was subsequently put into a corner regarding whether this phone call actually took place, but knowing the integrity and calibre of the people that were present when this call was made, I have no doubts.

The Loan to AI was fully disclosed as is required in the Financial Statements of TWOA for the years 2001, 2002, 2003 and 2004, as an 'Advance to Aotearoa Institute', and identified by a separate note in the Notes to Financial Statements, as evidenced by Note 13 to the Financial Statements section of the 2003 Annual Report.

These financial statements were audited by the Auditor General's contracted auditors (Deloitte), who issued unqualified audit reports for each of the years. Further the financial statements were also lodged with the Ministry of Education (a requirement of the Education Act). It should also be noted that the loan appeared in all Balance Sheets presented at the monthly Council meetings that the Crown appointed Development Advisor McNally, attended.

In hindsight, it would appear that the correct process was not followed by TWOA for this loan to AI, but no advice regarding this was ever received from the Ministry, who unsurprisingly, subsequently denied that that approval, albeit by telephone, was ever requested. Let's also be clear that AI had no use for this building; AI did not see itself as a property company, it merely did what was thought to be the best solution to benefit the students of TWOA.

The conclusion I draw from the above is that the Ministry of Education failed both its Minister and TWOA in respect of advice given regarding this advance by TWOA to its parent and founding body, to assist it to complete a purchase that was used solely for the benefit of TWOA students. If it was such an issue, why did it take four years to surface?

Criterion 33 – Failure to submit Business Plans

TEIs are not required to submit business plans, although there are very clear requirements to submit Profile and Charters. Under Section 159N and 159Y of the Education Act 1989, a TEI **cannot** receive EFTS funding without having prior approved Profiles and Charters. TWOA was receiving that funding, and has continued to up to today's date. Mallard was not even close on this one.

Criterion 34 – Continuance of Government Funding

This criterion relates to any business or entity that is almost solely dependent on the Crown for funding. Clearly changes in Government policies are always a risk to those reliant on such funding. Any downside risk to this would entirely be the responsibility of the state, and not a factor that a TEI should be held to account. This was a risk that was within Mallard and his Cabinet's power to control. Again, not even close.

Criterion 35 – The future Cash Flow issues

By June 2005, TWOA **did not** have cash flow issues, as Roache had arranged a Crown loan of up to $20 million. That was the same amount as the suspensory loan, and as we will find out, actually the same appropriated money, with a different name. However, this conveniently phased

Crown loan had different conditions applied to it that would have been attached to the suspensory loan. I repeat myself, again, not even close.

We will look at this Crown loan a little later, but not before I explain what Mallard saw through the small window that McNally, from his position of trust at TWOA, pointed to. What I mean, is how Mallard manipulated the suspensory loan process to get the leverage that McNally referred.

Chapter 10 – Suspensory loan

TWOA clearly and quite reasonably, anticipated the state honouring the terms of the Deed of Settlement relating to the suspensory loan. As will be shown, Council members, the Crown Development Advisor (McNally) and Ministry of Education all knew that this funding was important, if not critical.

Based on the recommendations of the Waitangi Tribunal, TWOA entered into two Settlement Deeds with the state. The first was referred to as Partial Settlement, and the second was the Final Settlement.

First Deed - Partial Settlement

Twenty-one months after the Waitangi Tribunal Report (Wai.718) came out, on 20th December 2000, the Crown and TWOA executed a Partial Settlement Deed. This Deed recognised part (a) of the Tribunal's recommendation, which was to compensate TWOA for past investment in land, buildings, plant and equipment, to the sum of $6.459 million, and the costs of bringing the claim, of $152,000. The Crown paid TWOA these sums on or about 23rd December 2001.

Second Deed - Final Settlement

Nearly a year later, on 6th November 2001, the Crown and TWOA executed the Final Settlement Deed, under which the Crown agreed to make payments to TWOA "sufficient to cover the cost of bringing its buildings, plant and equipment up to a standard comparable to other TEIs and commensurate with the needs of TWOA's existing and anticipated student rolls over the next three years". This Deed was in recognition of part (b) of the Tribunal's recommendations.

Clause 9 of the Settlement Deed states:

> "In respect of recommendation (b) of the Tribunal's report the Crown will as soon as reasonably practicable pay the claimant initial redress in the sum total of twenty-five million dollars ($25m) (excluding Goods and Services Tax ("GST"), if any, and excluding any income tax that may be payable). Additional redress will become due and payable upon the terms and conditions set out in Schedule A and payment shall be made at the times and in accordance with the conditions set out in Schedule A".

Under Schedule A of the Final Settlement Deed, the Crown agreed to pay TWOA $15 million dollars in 'additional redress' ($10 million in 2002 and $5 million in 2003), conditional upon the 'material achievement' of certain performance targets set out in clause 4 of Schedule A of the Settlement Deed. One of those performance targets was that "at least 80% of students will be Māori".

The payment of this additional redress is important in relation to negotiations for the release of the suspensory loan, as the payments were intended to be linked to the stated performance target. The Crown paid the 'additional redress' as follows:

1 February 2002 $4 million

1 July 2002	$6 million
13 March 2003	$3 million
1 July 2003	$2 million

In fact, the 2002 and 2003 Annual Reports of TWOA show that Māori student enrolments were 77% in 2002, and 59% in 2003. These did not meet the 80% performance target referred to above, but nevertheless the Crown paid to TWOA the full $40 million provided for in the Deed of Settlement, which included the 'additional redress' that was dependant on the 80% Māori percentage target.

The Final Settlement Deed also provided for a suspensory loan, payable when the terms and conditions set out in Clause 7 of Schedule A were met. In considering this suspensory loan, it should be noted that the amount of $40 million was established as what both parties to the negotiations believed to be appropriate at the time of the negotiations; that is up to November 2001. For the 2001 year, TWOA had 6,118 EFTS. The payment of $40 million therefore equates to about $6,500 per EFTS.

Pertinent aspects of Clause 7 of Schedule A are:

"7.1 In order to support the achievement of a higher growth path identified in negotiations with the wānanga, the Crown agrees to the provision of additional capital by way of a suspensory loan on the following terms and conditions:

7.1.1 In the event that the wānanga achieves a greater path such that EFTS enrolments reach the figure of 10,900 EFTS by 2003, then, subject always to the achievement and maintenance of high quality standards the Crown, acting by and through the Ministers of Finance and Education, will enter into a suspensory loan in the sum total of $20 million to be made available on a progressive basis to the wānanga commencing in the year 2004 and ending in the year 2006.

7.1.3 Subject to clause 7.1.1 the amount of the suspensory loan shall be payable in the following tranches:

- $10 million draw able in the calendar year 2004;
- $5 million draw able in the calendar year 2005;
- $5 million draw able in the calendar year 2006.

7.1.5 The Secretary for Education shall agree with the Wānanga the terms and conditions of the loan and the conditions for the conversion of the loan to equity. Agreements for the loan and a performance agreement (covering similar items to Clause 4 of this Schedule) for the period 2004 to 2006 shall be complete prior to the provision of loan monies".

The evidence provided to the Waitangi Tribunal, in respect of a claim made by AI in 2005 (Wai.1298), showed that in 2001, Cabinet agreed to seek appropriations from Parliament for the sum of $20 million under Vote-Education. Clearly, there was Cabinet approval as early as 2001 for a suspensory loan to be made available to TWOA, with $10 million payable in 2003/4, $5 million in 2004/5 and $5 million in 2005/6, provided always that TWOA met the requirements of in Clause 7.1 of Schedule A which related to EFTS numbers achieved. We know that TWOA blitzed these requirements. So did Mallard.

Let us now look at the process and progress of the negotiations between the state and TWOA in respect of the release of the suspensory loan proceeds, which took place during 2004, and see what is to be made of all of this. Remember in 2002, well before these negotiations commenced, TWOA had achieved over 20,000 EFTS, nearly double the Deed of Settlement Clause 7.1.1 'trigger' number of 10,900 EFTS that was set to be achieved by 2003.

Chapter 11 – The suspensory loan draw down progress

This chapter is full of important details. However, if you are not really interested in the detail, just the outcome, you are welcome to go to the summary at the end. If you want to understand how these things work, read on.

Let it be clear: TWOA met the conditions under clause 7.1.1 of Schedule A of the Final Settlement Deed that entitled it to receive the suspensory loan. It reached 20,769 EFTS in 2002 and 34,280 EFTS in 2003, while maintaining high quality standards.

The fact that TWOA wished to receive the suspensory loan was raised from time to time by TWOA after February 2004, first with a Senior Business Analyst at TAMU and then with the TWOA/MOE Liaison Officer of the Ministry of Education, Black. On 9th July 2004, Dr Wetere wrote to the Senior Policy Analyst at TAMU, formally requesting the release of $10 million to TWOA under the terms of the suspensory loan. He stated that TWOA believed it had achieved and exceeded all of the preconditions under the Final Settlement Deed and noted that the amount requested was to allow TWOA to fund current growth needs for 2004 and beyond.

There was no pressure on TWOA's liquidity at this time, or, as it will become apparent, at any time during the 2004 year. However, it was reported in evidence to the

Waitangi Tribunal in 2005 that the state misplaced, mismanaged or lost TWOA's July 2004 application for the loan until September 2004. Further, Dr Wetere stated at the Tribunal that as he had not received a response to the request for release of the loan, he arranged to meet with Mallard on 16th September 2004. In preparation for this meeting, on 9th September 2004 Dr Wetere wrote to Mallard stating that:

> "a) TWOA wanted to draw down the full $20 million that year because TWOA had grown well beyond 11,000 EFTS in size;
>
> b) TWOA had accelerated its acquisition of capital resources to better cope with student growth by utilising operational surpluses over the last two years; and
>
> c) One of the key factors in TWOA's success had been its endorsement by non-Māori students in New Zealand, who were likely to be 50% of TWOA's total student intake in 2004".

The importance of b) above should not be overlooked. Dr Wetere made it known to Mallard at this early stage, that TWOA had accelerated expenditure on capital "to better cope with student growth"; growth that must have been apparent to Mallard and the Ministry, as the Ministry heralded this in their 2003 report that has already discussed.

The Development Advisor, McNally, emailed the

Ministry of Education on 21st December 2004 that capital expenditure was over budget. He wrote:

> "Principal reasons for the change in the wānanga's financial situation included the fact the EFTS are down and that capital expenditure is likely to be 24 million dollars or 9 million dollars over budget".

It is absolutely clear that this additional expenditure on capital was signalled to Mallard in Dr Wetere's letter to him of 9th September 2004; it makes you wonder if Mallard ever bothered reading this. To put the "9 million dollars over budget" into perspective, it should be noted that the amount was $1 million less than the first drawdown of the suspensory loan understood by TWOA to have been due for payment on 1st July 2004.

Another key point of the 9th September 2004 letter from Dr Wetere, is that it signals to Mallard that non-Māori enrolments were likely to make up around 50% of the student enrolments for 2004. This issue of ethnic percentage became an important issue in the later stages of the negotiations for the release of suspensory loan, and I am not sure why this matter was not raised by Mallard in September 2004. Again, it makes you wonder if he reads these things.

It is evident that face to face negotiations for the release of the suspensory loan started on 13th October 2004 when the Manager of TAMU met with Dr Wetere at TWOA in Te Awamutu. The matters discussed, according to evidence presented to the Waitangi Tribunal in 2005, were:

"(a) The potential draw down of $20 million under the suspensory loan;

(b) The need to set and agree to key performance indicators before the suspensory loan release could be agreed;

(c) The Manager of TAMU undertook to look into the payment of $20 million in full;

(d) The Manager of TAMU indicated that it may be difficult to obtain the full $20 million in the near future because the dates for payment were stipulated in the Final Settlement Deed, but that $15 million should be released by the Crown as soon as the loan agreement was signed;

(e) The Manager of TAMU did not give any indication that there would be any problems completing the loan agreement or that there would be any difficult issues to work through; and

(f) The Manager of TAMU emailed response to the Tumuaki's letter of 9th July 2004 was discussed. This had not been received by TWOA, and the Manager of TAMU undertook to send it again".

All very positive; like minded people working together, as you would expect.

Following this meeting, on 20th October 2004, Dr Wetere wrote to the Manager of TAMU because TWOA had not received a formal response to its July application for the release of the suspensory loan. He stated:

"(a) TWOA's intention was to draw down the whole $20 million due under the suspensory loan at the earliest possible time because the first instalment of $10 million due in the 2004 calendar year had not been received;

(b) TWOA had continued with its capital development plan funded from surpluses generated from operating activities over the past three years;

(c) To maintain a strong financial position TWOA required a further injection of cash; and

(d) TWOA believed it had fulfilled the quality standards under the Final Settlement Deed, and in particular, had exceeded the growth targets".

Evidence presented to the Waitangi Tribunal (Wai.1298) state that in a paper dated 4th November 2004, the Tertiary Education Commission (TEC) advised Mallard and Maharey that:

"(a) The Minister of Education was to meet with the Tumuaki of TWOA on 11th November 2004 (rescheduled from 16th September 2004);

(b) The 2001 Final Settlement Deed provided for additional capital of $20 million to be provided by way of suspensory loan;

(c) The suspensory loan was conditional on TWOA achieving 10,900 EFTS by 2003 and achieving high quality standards;

(d) The Final Settlement Deed also contained a requirement that, should certain performance standards not be achieved, TWOA and the Crown would enter into a plan of action to address the variations from target;

(e) The terms and conditions of the suspensory loan would be agreed between TWOA and the Secretary for Education. This would include performance measures to be achieved. The performance measures were to cover similar criteria to the Final Settlement Deed for student numbers, student profile, educational outcomes, quality and financial performance;

(f) TAMU is currently in the process of preparing the suspensory loan agreement and reviewing the appropriate performance measures. This will then be discussed and agreed with TWOA; and

(g) Given the larger than expected growth in EFTs at TWOA, it has now sought the full payment of the suspensory loan as conveniently possible".

On 11th November 2004, Dr Wetere met with Mallard, Maharey and Ministry Officials. According to evidence presented to the Waitangi Tribunal in 2005, Maharey, the Minister of Tertiary Education no less, said that he understood TWOA had met the preconditions for payment of the suspensory loan and that "he was surprised that the amount due had not been paid".

It is quite clear from Dr Wetere's evidence to the Waitangi Tribunal that officials from the Ministry of Education and TWOA entered into prolonged negotiations on an agreement for the suspensory loan. Four meetings were held between the Ministry's liaison officer and TWOA during November and December 2004, and a Draft Performance Agreement was substantially agreed by the parties at meetings on 23rd November and 15th December 2004. In addition to the meetings referred to, email communications were extensive as is evidenced by what follows.

On 23rd November 2004, Black, the Ministry of Education liaison person for TWOA, emailed a 'Capital Contribution Agreement (Treaty Settlement) by way of Suspensory Loan Document – Draft Nov 2004', to TWOA. This document states in Clause 10: "The Crown agrees to advance the sum of $20 million (GST, not applicable) to the Wānanga, for the purposes specified in Clause 12. The document in the Schedule to the Suspensory Loan – Performance Agreement, sets out under Student Profile: Māori Students >50%".

On 23rd November 2004, the TWOA researcher handling this issue of the Performance Agreement reported to the management team of TWOA by email that he had met Black that afternoon, and that Black was quite amenable to most of the changes. On 26th November 2004, the researcher emailed the TWOA Management team again that Black had phoned and said that she had received feedback from the Māori Liaison person (at the Ministry of Education) who had concerns about the percentages of Māori students (which had been 86% in 2001, was now 46%) and that the Ministry contended that student ethnicity should be one of the main indicators of Wānanga success.

On 30th November 2004, the researcher emailed Black stating that the issue that appears to be causing most concern was the Māori student enrolment rate. He advised that TWOA had agreed to 60% under the Performance Agreement (excluding Kiwi Ora students) and added that if this was unacceptable, then they should meet again next week.

A file note of the researcher of 2nd December 2004, records a meeting with Black at Hamilton Airport on that date. It notes that Black stated:

> "$5 million should be released by Xmas.
> $10 million by early Feb.
> $5 million in July 05".

On 6th December 2004, the researcher emailed Black stating, "I was just wondering if you have made any progress with the Māori student indicators?" On 7th December 2004, Black emailed the researcher "not really and I think that we are going to have to do more work on this. I think a discussion with the Māori Tertiary Manager (of MOE) as well would be useful; hence a visit to Te Awamutu is necessary. The Manager is quite busy, so it may have to be the week commencing 20th December 2004".

On 8th December 2004, a Ministry of Education advisor (Sheppard) sent a memo to Black stating: "the Wānanga has an expectation that it will receive the loan monies having exceeded the EFTS figure". In respect of the suspensory loan, Sheppard wrote:

> "Point 13. My understanding from reading the summary of the claim and the report, the Deed is that the Wānanga is to receive a total of $60m as follows:
>
> - $25m when the Deed was signed (as compensation) for expenditure and labour by the Wānanga in the establishment process (no performance targets apply for this payment);
>
> - $15m in 4 instalments (as per the Capital Payment Schedule in the Deed - which is performance related as to EFTS, numbers of Māori students, and quality through retention, completion, and stair casing), this is for additional redress and is for improving premises to bring them up to the standard for other TEI's;
>
> - $20m as a suspensory loan over the period 1st January 2004 to 31st December 2006, this is for capital buildings etc. as a result of higher than projected growth. The loan may be for a period of 10 years i.e. to 31st December 2016 but that is not clear despite clause 7.1.4. It is also subject to performance targets of quality through retention, completion and stair casing. These conditions are to be negotiated with the Wānanga;

- The failure by the Wānanga of the performance targets (at least enrolment) for the $15m (which technically should not have been paid) may cause the Crown to consider negotiations of the $15m on a pro rata basis depending on the number of Māori students;

- The opportunity to negotiate is available to the Crown as a result of the conditions required to be included in the suspensory loan agreement and the performance agreement".

The above accepts that TWOA was to receive $60 million, of which $40 million had already been paid, and that a further $20 million was available "for capital buildings etc. as a result of higher than projected growth". It also points out that there was the opportunity available to the Crown to negotiate further in respect of this loan.

According to evidence presented to the Waitangi Tribunal (Wai.1298), on 10th December 2004, Sargison (the TAMU person we have already met) wrote to the Ministry of Education stating:

> "Rob came to me a few weeks ago and suggested that the process be slowed or alternatively that there be no hurry to provide the cash. As I said to him I can see no reason to delay. It may be that 80% Māori is the 'right' figure but I think we just made it up at the time".

The above statement that the process "be slowed" seems to confirm that there was dialogue within the

Ministry of Education that there should be "no hurry to provide the cash"; meaning of course, the suspensory loan proceeds, which most honourable people would agree were, by this stage, was due to TWOA.

In his evidence before the Waitangi Tribunal, Dr Wetere noted that the performance criteria that was the subject of negotiations, and he stated that at no point during the negotiations in November and December 2004, did Ministry of Education officials suggest that TWOA had failed to meet this precondition under the Final Settlement Deed that entitled it to receive the suspensory loan proceeds.

Dr Wetere also stated that on the 13th December 2004, a Noting Submission was sent to the Minister of Education proposing that Ministers would approve the payment of $5 million under the suspensory loan once performance measures were agreed and a suspensory loan agreement was signed. Attached to the Noting Submission, was a draft paper from Mallard to the Cabinet Social Development Committee, which sought approval to reappropriate $10 million for the suspensory loan from 2003/04 to 2004/05, because TWOA had not utilised the $10 million in the 2003/04 financial year. The reappropriations would have made available suspensory loan payments of $5 million in December 2004 (under the existing 2004/05 appropriation), $10 million in February 2005 (under the new 2004/05 appropriation) and $5 million in July 2005 (under the existing 2005/06 appropriation).

On 16th December 2004 the TWOA researcher

emailed the TWOA management team, advising that he had met with Black the day before, and that she advised that the process for the payment of the suspensory loan was underway.

But on 17th December 2004 (two days after the 15th December Council meeting, that will be discussed in the next chapter) McNally emailed the manager of TAMU (Sargison) advising him that the wānanga was forecasting a deficit of about $6 million over 2004, and that there was a minor risk of TWOA having to seek approval for borrowing in February or March 2005. We know what he then said, "just a small window to get some leverage". What a complete breach of trust!

You can see it all unfolding now. On 20th December 2004, McNally sought guidance from the Ministry of Education on the approval process for an overdraft borrowing facility. On the same day, the Finance Director of TWOA told the Ministry of Education contact person that whether or not they needed to borrow, was entirely dependent on when the suspensory loan proceeds were received. I cannot understand for one minute what mandate McNally thought that he had, to make the above request on behalf of TWOA, or why he even thought that it was any of his business. Was he acting in the best interests of TWOA?

On 21st December 2004, McNally emailed a manager employed at the Tertiary Education Commission and stated that there would be pressure on TWOA's cash flow position in January and February 2005. I question this. At this stage

TWOA were only going to be concerned about their cash position, if the suspensory loan proceeds of $5 million, were not going to be received. Therefore, what did McNally know on this date that TWOA did not?

Clearly, by this stage, Ministry officials and those at the Tertiary Education Commission were aware that TWOA might need permission to borrow if it did not get access to the suspensory loan funding. On 22nd December 2004, the issue was put beyond doubt. An email to McNally and Black from the Finance Director of TWOA stated:

> "The issue of whether or not we will have to borrow is very dependent on the timing of paying the suspensory loan. Can you please advise me of your expected dates and amounts for this?"

On 22nd December 2004, Black responded to the above email stating:

> "As I mentioned to the Council meeting last week, the release of the funds is based on a reasonable close agreement on the performance measures (i.e. we don't have to have signed the loan agreement – tho (sic) the deed actually says it has to be – but I think we can work round it – but I will need to check that with Bob). Richard and I have been in discussion regarding that – and we still have some issues with the Māori student profile. I now need to discuss this with the MoE senior managers (including the Chief Exec) to get a minimum that will be acceptable to MoE to meet the intent of the

treaty settlement".

Later in the day of 22nd, Black emailed the researcher at TWOA stating:

> "Here is a draft. As you can see the Māori profile is still an issue and at MoE we are still not convinced that 60% is acceptable. What is the process for you regarding getting management and Council sign off?"

The draft referred to was a Capital Contribution Agreement, that is, the agreed terms for suspensory loan, including when funds would be released.

On 18th January 2005, as Dr Wetere advised the Waitangi Tribunal (Wai.1298), TWOA's Executive Committee resolved to agree to the Capital Contribution Agreement between the state and TWOA, and signed it. This provided for payments by the State of $5 million in 2004 and $10 million in 2005, subject to certain performance measures. On the same day, Dr Wetere wrote to the Secretary for Education, attaching the signed Capital Contribution Agreement in anticipation of the Secretary for Education's acceptance, and he requested an immediate draw down of $5 million, as a matter of urgency. He stated that he expected that a further payment of $10 million or $15 million would be finalised at a meeting with the Secretary for Education scheduled for 2nd February 2005 in Wellington.

By 28th January 2005 the Ministry officials sought to impose more stringent performance requirements on

TWOA before the suspensory loan would be paid. Black sent a memo to the Secretary for Education that day and advised:

"(a) The Ministry had not been advised of the outcome of the meeting on 17th December 2004 between the Minister of Finance and Rongo Wetere;

(b) The initial application for the loan made in July 2004 had been lost by the Ministry due to staff movements;

(c) That in October 2004 TAMU had begun discussions with Aotearoa (sic) around the performance indicators to be attached to the loan agreement and that all indicators had been agreed except for the one which relates to the percentage of Māori students;

(d) It was the intention in early December to agree the performance indicators and release $5 million; this was not followed through because the performance indicators had not finally been agreed to;

(e) Rongo Wetere was in a 'grievance mode'; and

(f) Rongo Wetere commented that the Treaty relationship is a working partnership and the memorandum of agreement negotiated with the Crown in 2001 has not been ratified by the Crown. The Ministry is currently looking into this".

The same day (28th January 2005) Black sent a further memo to the Secretary of Education Fancy, which stated:

> "(a) The key performance indicators would include a new "governance" measure, which was not in the original Settlement Deed, and more explicit quality measures, although methodologies and targets were yet to be decided;
>
> (b) A higher proportion of Māori students were required, because:
>
> i) Given the definition of a Wānanga provided in the Act, and the intentions of the Settlement, officials are of the view that the proportion of Māori students should he higher (than currently is the case at TWOA):
>
> (ii) If the key performance indicators and loan agreement were agreed, TWOA would receive $15 million in February or March 2005 and $5 million in March 2006".

Dr Wetere gave evidence to the Waitangi Tribunal (Wai. 1298) that on 2nd February 2005, he met with the Secretary for Education Fancy, to discuss the suspensory loan. By then, despite the extensive negotiations throughout November and December 2004, Fancy had decided that TWOA did not yet meet the conditions that would 'trigger' their entitlement to the suspensory loan. He wrote to Dr Wetere stating that:

"I would like to assure you that I too am keen that we make progress and reach agreement on the suspensory loan, and the trigger points which convert it to equity in 2007".

He added:

"While I do not undervalue what TWOA is doing to meet the educational needs for non Māori, in the judgements I need to make, I need to assess KPI information relating to Māori participation and achievement".

Fancy also added that he was expecting a report from TAMU on actual performance against the performance indicators that would trigger the suspensory loan, so that he could judge that the performance criteria have been materially achieved. He concluded that once this was done to his satisfaction, the next step would be to agree terms of the suspensory loan and performance measures for conversion of the loan to equity in 2007.

As we know, Dr Wetere told the Waitangi Tribunal that on 22nd February 2005, seven days after the Shirley outbursts in parliament, Mallard wrote to TWOA advising of his concerns at the public profile of the wānanga (created by him?) and of increasing issues of performance and accountability. He followed this on 28th February 2005 with his Aide memoire, which to summarise stated:

"That as the wānanga have not met the conditions to access the suspensory loan, I will not be recommending to Cabinet that the wānanga be given access to the suspensory loan at this time".

The above makes it clear that from 28th February 2005, TWOA was not going to get the proceeds of the suspensory loan in the near or foreseeable future. This of course was Mallard's desired outcome, after he had been pointed to the small window by McNally. The rantings in parliament, under parliamentary privilege by Mallard's past Cabinet colleague Shirley, were just part of the justification process.

Chapter 12 – The relevance of the suspensory loan

Was there really a pending cash crisis for TWOA, and what actual cash balances did it hold during 2004, and through to June 2005? It was in this time period that the state claimed there would be a cash crisis for TWOA and justified to Mallard, that the state should take control of TWOA.

The TWOA Council Meeting Papers for the meeting on 15th December 2004, the Tumuaki noted in his report:

> "Negotiations have commenced with the Ministry of Education regarding a drawdown of the suspensory loan facility agreed to by the Crown in the Deed of Settlement. It is hoped that some funds may become available before the end of this year".

The Financial Report - November Results 2004 presented to the same meeting noted:

> "Cash balances at 30th November amount to $20.1m for the Group compared to forecast of $38.7m. The reforecast includes an expected reduction in funding to occur because we were not meeting the 32,000 funded levels. This reduction has not occurred and we have received an unexpected/unforecast $15m in funding included in the current $20.1m cash balance. The necessary

adjustment in funding received may not now take place until January 2005. The excess funding has temporarily inflated cash balances. Considerable increased expenses and the purchase of stocks and fixed assets have given rise to a greater than expected cash outflow".

Further:

"Working capital for the Group amounts to $8.5m. The Group currently has liability for MOE funding recorded at $13m. This liability is based on being funded for 29,796 efts to date compared to actual consumption to date of 27,471. This liability will reduce significantly as efts consumption increases although the expected return of funding has not yet occurred".

Further:

"Capital expenditure for the parent is now over budget. Total spend on fixed assets amounts to $23.1m and the total budget for 2004 is $15.4m. The additional spend on fixed assets will impact on the current estimated depreciation charge for 2004".

Further:

"The receipt of $5m in relation to the suspensory loan of $20m has not been forecast to occur until December. The cash flow on page 12 and graph on page 10 provides an estimated reforecast cash flow. Given continued high expenditure, cash balances are likely to fall to $22.9m (including the receipt of $5m suspensory loan) from a forecast of $40.7m".

A summary of the above is that there were no cash flow issues apparent for the eleven months ended 30th November 2004 or reported to the 15th December 2005 full Council meeting of TWOA, at which the state's Development Advisor McNally was present. However, ample warning was given as to the importance of receiving the suspensory loan funding in a timely manner. Page 11 of the Financial Report for November 2004 included with the Council Meeting Papers for the 15th December 2004 meeting, detailed actual cash closing balances for January 2004 to November 2004, shown in Table 6.

Table 6: Month end cash balances

Jan 2004 $34,000,000	**July 2004 $34,072,000**
February $33,923,000	**August $38,313,000**
March $39,775,000	**September $32,204,000**
April $34,275,000	**October $26,411,000**
May $31,560,000	**November $20,164,000**
June $31,642,000	**Dec (Budgeted) $22,889,000**

The figures shown in Table 6 have been calculated from a graph presented to the 15th December 2004 meeting. The actual figures may have varied from this interpretation of what these figures were, but any variance caused by interpretation would be insignificant.

The 2005 Budget included with the TWOA Council Meeting Papers for 15th December meeting also noted under Financial Report (part 2) stated:

> "Total income for TWOA is budgeted at $202m with a surplus of $8.87m generating a return on revenue of 4.37%. The earlier months of 2005 see a dramatic fall in cash balances. The return of efts funding is budgeted to take place in January and February (MOE funding based on 32,000 efts has been received) and a return of the excess funding will need to occur".

The Financial Report (Part 2) further stated:

> "This has a significant impact on the working capital of the organisation. However, provided budgeted targets are met the cash position will be improved towards the end of 2005. Given the repayment of funding, and capital spend; cash balances will fall from the opening position even given the receipt of the suspensory loan".

Further:

> "The receipt of the suspensory loan will be essential to the support of the wānanga. An initial $5m is budgeted to occur late December 04 and a further $10m of funds in (sic) budgeted to be received in April. The remaining $5m is not budgeted to occur until 2006".

The figures used in Table 7 on the following page, were submitted to the Council Meeting of 15th December 2004, showing the anticipated month end cash positions for the 2005 year.

Notes to the above Cash Flow – 2005 Budget were: (bold for emphasis)

- “Repayment of MOE funding budgeted to occur in January $12.8m.
- **Receipt of Suspensory Loan budgeted - $5m in Dec. 04 and $10m in April.**
- Cash Deficit for Parent budgeted to occur February/March”.

Table 7: Budgeted month end cash balances

	Group
December 2004	$22,500,000
January 2005	$10,000,000
February	$7,000,000
March	$6,000,000
April	$14,000,000
May	$18,000,000
June	$22,000,000
July	$27,000,000
August	$32,500,000
September	$31,500,000
October	$28,000,000
November	$26,000,000
December	$20,000,000

Table 7 shows no cash deficits predicted for the Group for 2005. It should be noted that TWOA was the parent, and that the group included MO1 Limited, a fully owned subsidiary of TWOA, that run the highly profitable Mahi

Ora programme.

Certainly no dramas here are there **IF** the suspensory loan proceeds were received in December 2004, and April 2005.

However Table 8 shows cash deficits for the Group in January to April 2005, **if the suspensory loan proceeds were not received** when they were budgeted to be. The red (bracketed) figures mean borrowings.

Table 8: Budgeted month end case less Suspensory Loan

	Group – Budget as Table 7	Less: Sus Loan
Dec 2004	$22,500,000	$17,500,000
Jan 2005	$10,000,000	($5,000,000)
February	$7,000,000	($8,000,000)
March	$6,000,000	($9,000,000)
April	$14,000,000	($1,000,000)
May	$18,000,000	$3,000,000
June	$22,000,000	$7,000,000
July	$27,000,000	$12,000,000
August	$32,500,000	$17,500,000
September	$31,500,000	$16,500,000
October	$28,000,000	$13,000,000
November	$26,000,000	$11,000,000
December	$20,000,000	$5,000,000

Note: – Red (brackets) denotes deficit and Sus Loan is suspensory loan.

This clearly is what McNally picked up on, and what he couldn't seem to get back fast enough to his office, to tell Sargison about. Hold back the suspensory loan and there is a small window for some leverage?

As we know, almost to the point of nausea, on 17th December 2004, the Development Advisor (McNally) emailed the head of TAMU, Sargison, that TWOA would be pressure on the cash flow position in January and February. Chen Palmer 'Key Documents from Ministry of Education relating to the suspensory loan' memo of 26th July 2005, gives greater insight on the 17th December 2004 email from McNally. It included the following statements:

"(a) A deficit of up to 6 million dollars was reported to the December Council meeting of the wānanga, the deficit will probably end up in the range of 4 million to 9 million.

(b) Principal reasons for the change in the wānanga's financial situation included the fact the EFTS are down and capital expenditure is likely to be 24 million dollars or 9 million dollars over budget; and

(c) There will be pressure on the cash flow position in January and February 2005.

In summary, TWOA is forecasting a deficit of about 6 million dollars over 2004. There is a minor risk of TWOA having to seek approval for borrowing in Feb/Mar. Rongo was very conciliatory and concerned – how could this have occurred?!! (sic). He wants to discuss some issues in early January. I pushed the line of the impact on reputation and the risk of Crown intervention – particularly if borrowing approval was required – this struck a cord (sic) with Rongo. Happy to give me (sic) details - **just a small window to get some leverage"** (my emphasis).

Now what is McNally saying here? "A deficit of about $6 million dollars over 2004". I was at that meeting, and I have already provided details of what was reported to that meeting regarding finances. Even if McNally's assumptions were correct, in view of some nearly $60 million in profits (surpluses) over 2002 and 2003, most accountants, would described a $6 million deficit, as immaterial. McNally also refers to a "minor risk of TWOA having to seek approval to borrow in Feb/Mar". I do not know how McNally believes that he had the right to say this on 17 December 2004. This situation was not shown in the TWOA budgets. What was shown were balances that clearly showed what TWOA expected and predicted; that is, the receipt of the suspensory loan proceeds in an ethical and timely manner, with resulting cash balances as demonstrated in Table 7.

However McNally did work out, apparently with no concern to the best interests of the Council that he was supposed to serve, was that if Mallard procrastinated with the release of the suspensory loan proceeds, then there would be "just a small window to get some leverage". As I see it ,McNally flew in the face of all that I respected of my old firm Deloitte; acted completely against my understanding of the *Code of Ethics* of the Institute that I believe that we both belonged, and in my opinion, sold himself short on all and every principle of good governance practices.

Chen Palmer state in their 'Key Documents from Ministry of Education relating to the Suspensory Loan' that the 17th December 2004 email from McNally cites two emails from a recently appointed Crown member to the TWOA Council regarding poor council processes, and in respect of the 2004 year end result. The writer of those emails said:

> "To be fair I would simply say that TWOA is not the only Council which has found itself in this situation – that goes right to the heart of the capability issues we talk of".

The author was the CEO of a regional TEI, who appeared to understand capability issues that regionally based institutions had to face.

I have already asserted that there was no "deficit of up to 6 million dollars reported to the December Council meeting of wānanga". I have already explained to you why capital expenditure was $9 million over budget. McNally seems to flick glibly between revenue and capital terminology when referring to "deficit" and changes in TWOA's financial situation. To reiterate, the reasons that capital expenditure was over budget was due to TWOA significantly exceeding student numbers anticipated at the time the Final Settlement Deed was negotiated.

Unpredicted student numbers were the core reason why the suspensory loan was introduced into the Final Settlement Deed, as it was recognised by both parties to the agreement, that more student numbers required more capital to support them. TWOA made a decision not to hold back on capital expenditure and funded the additional capital expenditure (the library remember; recommended by the Secretary of Education, Fancy), from reserves, with the understanding that this additional capital expenditure would be covered by the proceeds of the suspensory loan.

Put another way, TWOA did not want to tell students to go home and come back when TWOA had received the suspensory loan proceeds. Furthermore, it would have been illegal for TWOA to accept EFTS funding, without resourcing students in accordance with the NZQA requirements for the course that the student had enrolled.

Things now get confusing in respect of the suspensory loan. According to evidence presented to the Waitangi Tribunal in relation to Wai.1298, a briefing paper to Mallard on 25th February 2005 (three days before Mallard's Aide memoire) states:

> "It is important to understand that there is a strong likelihood that TWOA will not exhibit any significant financial distress indicators later this year".

Further:

> "Any intervention based on financial distress might therefore be very short-lived and indeed could be open to some challenge in that the current situation is not too dissimilar to that faced by many TEIs at some point or other".

This did not seem to influence Mallard. Three days later, on 28th February 2005, out goes the Aide memoire to Cabinet completely ignoring what was in the briefing paper.

As a matter of record, the actual cash balances

reported by TWOA during late 2004 to December 2007 that I have been able to trace are shown in Table 9. Against these, are those calculated in Table 8, which shows would happen without the proceeds of the suspensory loan. Again, red or (brackets) is a deficit.

Table 9: Actual cash balances – Nov 2004 – Dec 2007

	Cash	Source	Table 8
Nov 2004	$20,164,000	Council	
Dec 2004	$14,666,000	Audited F/S	$17,500,000
March 2005	$4,650,000	Council	($9,000,000)
April 2005	$5,320,000	Council	($1,000,000)
May 2005	$10,590,000	Council	$3,000,000
Dec 2005	$9,816,000	Audited F/S	$5,000,000
Dec 2006	$5,469,000	Audited F/S	
Dec 2007	$21,861,000	Audited F/S	

Note: F/S is financial statements – audited. Red (brackets) - denotes deficit.

This table shows that TWOA received funds from somewhere, as there is a $13,650,000 increase in predicted funds at 31st March 2005 ($9,000,000 deficit), and those actually held at that date, $4,650,000 surplus. The question is, if the suspensory loan proceeds were not released, as Mallard said they wouldn't be, from where did these funds come?

Clearly, Roache would not have come to TWOA at $90,000 per month if he did not have some sort of guarantee that he would get paid. What he came with I believe, was an agreement that Mallard would front with some 'other funding' while all the rough stuff was going on. This funding, as we shall learn, was nicely referred as a Crown loan. Let's take a look.

In the Statement of Financial Position of TWOA as at 31st May 2005, which were part of the Council papers for their meeting of 28th June 2005, showed a bank overdraft of $12 million, and at the same date, funds at the bank of $10.590 million. Since TWOA had to get permission to borrow to that extent, we must assume that they did get permission, and borrowed.

At 31st December 2005, the audited financial statements of TWOA show Cash at Bank at $9.816 million and a liability referred to as Crown loan of $6 million. The Statement of Cash Flows for the year ended 31st December 2005, presented in the audited financial statements for that year, shows that funds were received from a Crown loan of $12 million and that the cash was applied to a settlement of debt of $6.014 million. In view of the fact that the Statement of Financial Position shows a liability of a Crown Loan at 31st December 2005, I conclude that before 31 May 2005, a bank overdraft of $12 million was negotiated, then repaid by a Crown loan of the same amount, and then, before 31st December 2005, $6 million of that loan was repaid.

The Crown loan of $12 million was $3 million less than

the amounts of the suspensory loan that the Final Settlement Deed scheduled to be due for payment well before the date that the Crown Loan was made!

The audited financial statements of TWOA for the year ended 31st December 2007 show, by way of the Cashflow Statement, that the balance of the 'Crown loan' was repaid during the financial year ended 31st December 2007. So at 31st December 2007, there was no Crown loan liability. Therefore, in the absence of the state honouring the terms of the Deed of Settlement in respect of the suspensory loan, the state made available $12 million to TWOA in May 2005. Obviously $6 million was repaid by 31st December 2005 and the balance by 31st December 2007. But by that date, the suspensory loan monies had yet been received by TWOA.

Chen Palmer (in their memo of 26th July 2005, 'Key Documents from Ministry of Education relating to the suspensory loan') suggest that the strategy behind the state's actions in denying the suspensory loan, but making available a Crown loan, was demonstrated by a paper entitled *Te Wānanga o Aotearoa – update on requirement for Crown assistance*, dated 29th April 2005, written by Allan Sargison of TAMU. Paragraph 15 of the Sargison paper states "the Council would have no option other than to agree to a short term loan from the Crown, and the conditions attached to it". Can you believe this?

The Crown loan did of course come with conditions that were not part of the Final Settlement Deed – suspensory loan clauses. These were:

“a) A restriction on TWOA selling assets, raising funds or granting security;

a) Regular reporting to the Ministry including monthly accounts, fortnightly update report on finances and operations, and weekly cash flow forecasts;

b) Continued appointment of the Crown Manager and payment of all of Crown Manager’s costs;

c) TWOA gives the Crown Manager power of attorney in relation to all matters governed by the Crown loan agreement and indemnifies the Crown and Crown Manager against any costs they incur arising from the exercise of the powers under the Crown loan agreement;

d) Introducing new procedures to improve governance and management accountability, reporting and performance;

e) Authorisation for the Crown to discuss TWOA’s financial affairs with TWOA’s auditors, advisers and bankers, and

f) A second ranking security interest (behind the Bank of New Zealand) in favour of the Crown”.

What a total change of rules.

Roache with control of the cheque book to ensure his $90k per month (ongoing for over three years to manage this); the state looking like a ‘white knight’ hero by providing a Crown loan that was in fact the suspensory loan allocated funds with a different name and conditions, and Council not only disempowered, but those who remained (several resigned in disgust), very much servants of the state.

Just to get this part right: the Statement of Claim in respect of Wai.1298 noted that the Crown loan was approved for $20 million, (the same amount as the withheld suspensory loan), and was paid from the previously approved Cabinet appropriation for the suspensory loan. So the Crown loan was the same money, from the same approved source, that was meant to be the suspensory loan. What made things different were the conditions attached to the Crown loan but certainly were not part of the suspensory loan!

By way of summary: TWOA did need the proceeds of the suspensory loan paid in a timely manner for the reasons agreed to in the first place. Without the proceeds of the suspensory loan, TWOA would have likely had to seek permission from the Secretary of Education to borrow up to $4 million in early 2005. With McNally's alert, Mallard decided to renege on payment of the suspensory loan. He then created a series of false reasons why he should, using mis-information provided to the public, through his past Cabinet member colleague, Shirley. He followed this by then putting in his man Roache in control of TWOA, and then agreed to advance to TWOA the same money that should have been the suspensory loan, with a different name and of course, with very punitive conditions attached.

Colonialism in full swing!!

Chapter 13 – The Auditor General's thoughts

What has surprised me over the years is the number of desperate people who demand audits when things don't seem to be going their way. Personally, I have never seen why anyone should be wary of a darned good auditing. However, like the desperate people that I refer to above, those that demand these audits, I think believe that they are about to unleash an unpleasant experience on the person/entity to be audited.

In the shrill February 2005 'softening up' of TWOA in parliament by Shirley, Mallard told the public that the Auditor General (OAG) would be investigating TWOA to look at "funding being channelled into subsidiary companies run by Wetere and family members"; and he "expressed serious concern about the institution, which has become the focus of allegations of financial extravagance and misuse of taxpayers' money".

He added:

> "I have concerns about that. My former Associate Minister, Steve Maharey, indicated that he had concerns about it. That is why the Auditor-General is looking into it. I think the Auditor-General is the appropriate person to look into conflicts of interest in tertiary institutions".

Of course that is what happened. It should be understood that the Office of the Auditor General is no one's pushover; it is a highly competent organisation with extensive powers and is respected at the highest levels of Government. As instructed, the A team arrived in Te Awamutu to conduct an investigation into 'certain aspects' of TWOA, against a background of extremely serious allegations made in Parliament, that clearly suggested major corruption and 'rorts', with clear inferences of scandal of the highest order. With access to top level accounting and legal personnel and very broad powers to obtain information, the Auditor General's report became a much anticipated and important document.

The Terms of Reference for the Auditor General's inquiry, set out on page 82 of his report, state:

> "Since September 2004, the Auditor General has been inquiring into potential conflicts of interest in relation to the Kiwi Ora programme at Te Wānanga o Aotearoa. As a result of this preliminary work, some other issues emerged. Further allegations have since been raised in the public domain, some of which have been the subject of requests for the Auditor General to extend his inquiry. The terms for this inquiry were to include:
>
> > 1) Procurement policies and practices, focusing on selected transactions where TWOA Councillors, employees and/or their close relatives are involved.

2) International travel policies.

3) Selected payments made to Councillors and/or employees of TWOA in relation to their involvement with entities controlled by TWOA.

4) Management of conflict of interests by TWOA in relation to Mahi Ora, Kiwi Ora and Green light programmes.

5) The relationship and transactions between TWOA and AI and its subsidiaries.

6) The implementation of TWOA's capital acquisition strategy.

7) Processes used by TWOA when employing close relatives of the Tumuaki.

8) Other issues that the Auditor General considers relate to or arise out of the above matters".

Although the Auditor General's report is headed 'Inquiry into certain aspects of Te Wānanga o Aotearoa, the catch-all paragraph 8) gave him the power to investigate almost any issue that might involve financial mal-practice.

The Auditor General began his investigation proper with an initial visit by members of his office and TEC, to TWOA in Te Awamutu on 6th and 7th April 2004. On 23rd April 2004, a team of three accountants and a lawyer representing the office arrived in Te Awamutu to commence their examination of records of TWOA and of AI. The results of the investigations were published in the Auditor General's report of 1st December 2005.

In the first section of that report, the Auditor General outlines the background as to why he decided there was a need for the inquiry, and he specifically refers to the allegations made by the Honourable Ken Shirley and certain media reports. He then sets out what his inquiry looked at, under the terms of reference.

On the second page of his Summary the Auditor General had completed his preamble and made his first observation. This one line read:

"We found practices that are unacceptable for a public entity".

This statement was immediately followed by:

> "However, the many negative comments in this report are explained by the selective nature of our inquiry. We have not conducted a comprehensive review of all of TWOA's activities, but have reported only on issues of significant concern within the areas we examined. We do not want to detract unnecessarily from TWOA's undoubted achievements".

My detailed examination of the Auditor General's report did not find any comments on any transactions that bear any resemblance to the allegations and media reports that he stated played a large part in extending the nature of his inquiry. The report did identify weaknesses in processes. In view of the fact that the organisation had grown so fast, this is not surprising.

For objectivity's sake, I analyse what I considered to be the negative and positive aspects of the Auditor General's report. Let's look at the negative first.

The reports said:

- "My inquiry into Te Wānanga o Aotearoa (TWOA) found practices that are unacceptable for a public entity. I found poor record-keeping and a consistent lack of documentation. What documentation I did see was often incomplete.
- Three themes were common to many of the activities I looked at:
    - poor decision-making practices for significant expenditure;
    - inadequate identification and management of conflicts of interest;
    - unacceptable practices in senior management expenses concerning international travel and credit card expenditure.
- TWOA and the Aotearoa Institute Te Kuratini o Nga Waka Trust Board (the AI Trust), a private organisation, have a close and ongoing business relationship, which dates back to TWOA's establishment. It covers many

different transactions, some of which are informal and unclear. I am concerned that TWOA has an unhealthy dependency on the AI Trust. TWOA could be left in a vulnerable position should its relationship with the AI Trust deteriorate or end. This creates significant risks for TWOA and its stakeholders.

- I consider that many of the individuals involved in TWOA have not appreciated the need to act with a public sector mindset.
- TWOA grew rapidly and significantly in recent years. During this time, it did not put in place appropriate systems and processes for such a large operation. Work is now being done on new policies and procedures, but it is taking too long to embed them into the culture and everyday practices of TWOA.
- TWOA needs to bring the same level of commitment to using its public resources responsibly as it has to pursuing its educational vision.
- Practices like those discussed in my report can be very damaging to the credibility of the public entity involved".

On Positive aspects the report said:

- "We note that the TWOA personnel we encountered displayed a strong commitment to, and passion for, TWOA, its educational goals, and its activities.

- However, the many negative comments in this report are explained by the selective nature of our inquiry. We have not conducted a comprehensive review of all of TWOA's activities, but have reported only on issues of significant concern within the areas we examined.
- We do not want to detract unnecessarily from TWOA's undoubted achievements.
- Work is now being done on new policies and procedures, but it is taking too long to embed them into the culture and everyday practices of TWOA.
- TWOA has enabled thousands of learners to have a second chance at education.
- I encourage central government agencies to consider carefully whether further guidance for, and monitoring of, tertiary education institutions is appropriate".

The Auditor General stated that he selected specific practices and transactions, and looked mainly at 2002, 2003, and 2004. He noted that in the last five years, TWOA had grown rapidly, from just over 1,000 students in 1999, to by 2003 having 63,387 students enrolled (equating to 34,280 equivalent full-time students) and 1,232 equivalent full-time staff. Measured in enrolments, he noted that TWOA had become the largest tertiary education institution in New Zealand.

A key observation by the Auditor General was:

> "During this time, it did not put in place appropriate systems and processes for such a large operation. Work is now being done on new policies and procedures, but it is taking too long to embed them into the culture and everyday practices of TWOA".

This was the big problem for TWOA; one encountered by many fast growing businesses. It was compounded by the difficulty that TWOA had in attracting staff to a small provincial town in rural Aotearoa New Zealand during the years 1999 to 2003, to keeping up with the demand of students as they chose to enrol with TWOA. The development of policies and procedures to match this growth was an issue, but this seemed to be acknowledged by the Associate Minister of Education in his 13th October 2004 letter, when he wrote:

> "The establishment of Audit and Risk Committee - strong Chair (John Storey) and independent member (Shane Jones) have been driving the development of a range of new policies and reviewing others, e.g. financial delegations, credit card usage, procurement etc. I understand they intend to move to a board risk analysis in the future".

John Story (JD) is another who is no light-weight. He was at one time Chair of the NZ Cooperative Diary Company, then Executive Chair. One time President of the NZ Institute of Directors; a Director of BNZ (Bank of New

Zealand) for 14 years, and Chair of the BNZ Audit & Risk Committee. I have said enough to establish his credentials. JD is a Te Awamutu man through and through, and without hesitation, when asked to head the TWOA Audit & Risk Committee, agreed.

This was a very intense time for the Audit & Risk Committee. It met monthly, simply running as fast as could be reasonably possible to get policies and procedures written by TWOA staff, and then adopted; while these staff members still had to deliver to the huge number of students. JD did this not at not anywhere near the rate of nearly $5,000 per working day that Roache and his team charged TWOA, I can assure you.

Shane Jones is no one's fool in the commercial scene either. Harvard educated, one time Chair of Sanfords Fisheries and of the Māori Fisheries Commission. These two gentlemen are at the top of the tree from a governance angle, and I believe that the Audit & Risk Committee, with their guidance, was essentially succeeding in doing the right thing from the governance point of view. Again, Shane did this at not anywhere near the rate of nearly $5,000 per working day that Roache and his team charged TWOA.

The Auditor General's only comment regarding conflicts of interest was that TWOA was inadequate in identifying and management of conflicts of interests. Funnily enough, the AOG did not comment on McNally's conflict of interest, but of course McNally had resigned from his position as Development Advisor well before the date of the OAG report.

In respect of the public allegations such as "funding being channelled into subsidiary companies run by Wetere and family members"; "misuse of taxpayers' money"; "rorts"; "one of the major programmes was developed by a staff member and sold to the wānanga for $7 million", and "all the same people are cross-pollinating these companies", "clipping the taxpayers' ticket", and "rorting the taxpayers of this country", the AOG had nothing to say. Do you think he would have if any of the above was vaguely correct? He certainly had the powers to do so, under paragraph 8) of his Terms of Reference.

The Auditor General stated in his report: "I encourage central government agencies to consider carefully whether further guidance for, and monitoring of, tertiary education institutions is appropriate". The matter of guidance and monitoring provided by central government agencies to TWOA was addressed by the Waitangi Tribunal in their report, Wai. 1298, and will be addressed in the next chapter.

I worked very closely with the Auditor General's team during this investigation. I found them to be decent people to deal with, professional in every way. I guess they seldom get thanks. To them I would like to say a thank you for the respect you showed to TWOA staff, to the kaupapa of TWOA, and for their compassionate handling of a tricky situation.

Chapter 14 - Aotearoa Institute responds

Aotearoa Institute (AI) took a hammering as well. There were all sorts of innuendo regarding the associations between TWOA and AI, with really unhealthy connotations. Remember, AI was the original training provider. It is a charitable trust created in 1983, and its activities in 1993, were assumed by the newly created wānanga, TWOA. AI transferred lock stock and barrel to TWOA, free of charge; all staff, resources, use of IP, use of vehicles, buildings and infrastructure. Effectively, AI backed out of delivering education.

AI did retain ownership of the land and buildings they had acquired prior to 1993, but it was some time before reasonably commercial rental agreements were put in place between AI and TWOA. AI Trustees did recognise that they had obligations as Trustees to see that things were relatively commercial. However, AI saw no reason to ask TWOA (a publically owned entity) to use scarce capital to pay AI to purchase its buildings, even after the Waitangi Tribunal decisions that prompted the 2001 and 2002 capital contributions under Settlement Deeds between TWOA and the state.

Clearly, AI always wished the best for TWOA, and did everything that it could to assist TWOA in its development. Predictably, the Trustees of AI did not reacted very well to what Mallard was up to in 2005, and as a result, requested an hearing, under urgency, at the Waitangi Tribunal. This was granted in September 2005 and here is what the Waitangi Tribunal had to say, after hearing all of the evidence from Al and the Crown.

The Waitangi Tribunal reported on Claim Wai.1298 in December 2005 - chapter 5: *Conclusions, Findings, and Recommendation*.

Summary of Findings. (My underlines for emphasis).

"(d) We find that the claim is well-founded in that the Crown has breached the principles of the Treaty in failing to protect the Rangātiratanga of TWOA as a Wānanga, with resulting prejudice to the claimants, by:

(i) attempting to define wānanga in such a way as to confine wānanga to the teaching of te reo and matauranga Māori to a predominantly Māori student body and attempting to force TWOA to comply with that mistaken definition through the charter process;

(ii) failing to ensure that a partnership/relationship agreement was concluded with TWOA in accordance with the Wai.718 deed of settlement;

(iii) failing to ensure that continuing consultation and negotiation took place between TWOA and the Crown at the level of the council and the Minister for Tertiary Education and Secretary for Education, so that issues could be dealt with appropriately;

(iv) failing to make adequate allowance in its dealings with this wānanga for TWOA's vulnerability due to the disproportionate effect of the growth cap, the various reviews, and the timeframes for compliance imposed on the wānanga;

(v) failing to ensure that the founding iwi, in particular, and other communities associated with the wānanga were given adequate opportunity to consult on changes to the charter of TWOA by insisting on an unusually tight timeframe;

(vi) putting TWOA in a position where council members resigned in an attempt to avoid the appointment of a commissioner, leading to a council that could not undertake consultation with iwi and other stakeholders;

(vi) failing to ensure that Crown agencies dealing with TWOA acted in a coherent and properly co-ordinated way and in accordance with an ongoing Treaty relationship; and

(vii) failing to ensure that Crown agencies implemented the various reviews with understanding of the protection and support that the Crown ought to provide for wānanga".

In short, the Waitangi Tribunal found that the Crown

acted in a manner that it should not have done under the Treaty, and that many of the Crown's actions, were harmful to TWOA.

These failings by the Crown, would appear to have been recognised by the Auditor General and prompted his comments: "I encourage central government agencies to consider carefully whether further guidance for, and monitoring of, tertiary education institutions is appropriate". The Tribunal's observation were that the Crown "failed to ensure that continuing consultation and negotiation took place between TWOA and the Crown, so that issues could be dealt with appropriately", would appear to be a direct reference to the protracted negotiation concerning the suspensory loan, and its eventual, non-payment.

The Auditor General's report was supportive of TWOA, while recommending management and policy improvements. The Waitangi Tribunal - Wai. 1298 report was also supportive of TWOA, and critical of the Crown. However, by the time that the both reports were made public, the state had control of TWOA, and Dr Wetere had resigned his position.

Chapter 15 – Summing up

Dr Rongo Wetere resigned as Tumuaki of TWOA in October 2005, when agreement was reached that his deputy, Bentham Ohia would take over as CEO. His position had clearly become untenable, his reputation, totally unjustly, destroyed, and the publicity was impacting on his family.

The reality is that the state, at I believe the highest level, wanted Dr Wetere out of TWOA. His tenacity, when faced with officials and Ministers, who would not accept his view that both Māori and non- Māori, were entitled to what TWOA provided, proved far too strong for the weak people that he was forced to deal with.

The normal, commercial outcome of the type of accusations made against the competencies that TWOA supposedly lacked, is a major restructuring; a complete clean out by a new broom. This did not happen after Dr Wetere had resigned. His deputy took over the lead role at TWOA, and is still in that position. His Finance Director is still the Finance Director, and it is the same for most management positions, including one of his sons remaining in a key leadership role.

A reconstructed Council was formed, filling the positions vacated by loyal long time Councillors (who thought that they doing the right thing for TWOA; not understanding that their resignations were exactly what Mallard wanted), with those who no doubt had a lot to contribute to the 're-focused' model. Roache and his team must have contributed something for $90,000 per month for three years from TWOA's funds. I am not sure they did any better than TWOA could and would have done on their own accord, with the over $3 million in fees paid to PWC, and the further $3 million that I understand was paid to the Auditor General's office.

Eventually, the suspensory loan was paid, in fact after the Crown loan had been repaid, and well after it was actually needed. My research shows that in 2011, TWOA had cash reserves in excess of $50 million. TWOA currently has some 12,000 EFTS, compared with its peak of 34,500. It has, like all other TEIs, a 'cap' on enrolments and now in Aotearoa New Zealand, no new course can enrol more than 200 students; a far cry from the several thousand that enrolled under the TWOA programmes.

I think that it should be understood that as far as I am aware, no one at TWOA in the early days, thought that it would attract anywhere near the student numbers that it did. In fact, for several years TWOA struggled with the notion that 1,500 EFTS seemed to be required in order to be viable. That TWOA achieved 34,500 EFTS in 2003 proved that there was a huge need and desire for tertiary education by, people previously seen to be disenfranchised from this sector, and who wished to better their lives. Dr Wetere's view was, "if the student knocks on our door. We will open it for them."

To the 'players' that I have referred; you know who you are, you know what you did, and I guess ultimately, you have to live with yourselves. The tragic thing is that in my experience, most of you will not even understand what sort of people you really are, and merely treated your roles as necessarily a part of a process. In my world, the attacks on Dr Wetere and his family, and the dubious processes that you all contributed to, are cowardly and an absolute shame to you all.

What then is there to learn from all of this?

The state clearly has unbridled power, which should, in a western democracy, be held in place by checks and balances. The reality is that the state has the power to do as it saw fit with TWOA. However, what does it say of the state if the reputations of fine, law abiding citizens, mean nothing? In my opinion, the state abused its power in relation to the way it treated Dr Wetere and his family, and as a consequence, TWOA.

The state apparatus does not function by itself. It needs Ministers, bureaucrats, and seemingly private sector 'consultants' to do their biddings. In the case of the state's battle for TWOA, the relationship between a bureaucrat (Sargison - merely doing his job I presume) and McNally (breach of trust at the highest level, in my opinion) proved to be too much for the humble folk at TWOA to comprehend.

Add to this, the platform that parliamentary privilege gives to those who, without any compunction whatsoever, can set out and completely destroy the reputations of people who score very high on every measure of human decency and merit. Dr Wetere is, and has always been, a very highly principled person: he had no right of reply, and as a result, no means to defend himself, and he was unable to call Shirley to account for his wide and damaging accusations.

Another point is what appears to me to be 'jobs for the boys'. Gardiner, McNally and Roache, are what have been described to me as private sector 'mercenaries'. They all, not unnoticed, went on to better and greater things after their roles in destroying reputations at TWOA. I do concede that Roache was just doing a job, but then I wonder what he really thought about the ethics of switching the money appropriated for the suspensory loan, to the Crown loan and then back again. Is this just the reality of big business and politics? Roache now is CEO of a very large SOE, again reporting to government.

Sargison has gone on to be the CEO of a tertiary institution of which McNally is the Chair. Which appointment came first, I wonder. The one thing all of these 'highly successful' people seem to have in common, as far as I can see, is their associations with TWOA. Maybe, in Wellington, that on your CV is the 'edge'.

Of McNally? He was a partner in the accounting firm that I hold in high regard. They are my alumni. My observations of him while he was in Te Awamutu, were that he did seem to consider himself a little better than the people that he was meant to be advising. In my opinion, he should never have taken on the role of Development Advisor to TWOA while his firm were also the auditors, and I believe his ultimate resignation from the role, acknowledged this fact.

As a consequence, in my opinion, he showed complete disregard for the *Code of Ethics* of the New Zealand Institute of Chartered Accountants in respect of independence, (certainly, as I read them) that I thought that he was bound. I have no doubt that good governance practices taught by his prestigious business school, would have clearly pointed out the fiduciary duty that I believe he owed to Councillors of TWOA. Predictably, he did not show his face back in Te Awamutu after he had discharged his duty to the Ministry of Education, and pointed them to the small window.

Of Sir Wira? Dr Wetere has a little more of his history with TWOA in the next section. Quite a history I say. However, from his brief appearance at TWOA in 2005, then to head of the Tertiary Education Commission, and then the gong! As my great mentor Ranginui said, "who would want to be in that company?"

Of the Honourable Ken Shirley? Clearly lacking the conviction or confidence to make any of his very serious allegations outside of parliament. Now gone from politics.

Of the Honourable Trevor Mallard? Much the same as for Shirley, but still there.

Dr Wetere Speaks

"I recall on my return to New Zealand in September 2011, at the Powhiri in Te Awamutu Apakura Campus ; Hirini Mead of Te Wananga o Awanuiarangi, publically acknowledged my contribution to Awanuiarangi. He said, "Rongo, We owe you a great debt of gratitude". That comment was a long time coming.

In 1994, Awanuiarangi was invited to join with Te Wananga o Aotearoa and Raukawa Wananga to form the Nga Tauihu o nga Wananga, an association that would help that iwi to gain status as a wānanga. We provided advice to Awanuiarangi's then CEO, the late Himiona Nuku. Wira Gardiner (who later became the Council Chair of Awanuiarangi) was at the time CEO to Te Puni Kōkiri (TPK). He knew that TPK had commissioned a confidential report on wānanga that in effect said that without capital of at least $10 million, each wānanga were not likely to succeed.

After years of unsuccessful applications for capital funding through the 1990s, a Ministry of Education Advisor quietly said to me, "Rongo, you need to make a request under the Official Information Act and you will find out who is holding up on your funding application." I discovered that the Secretary for the Ministry of Education wrote on our file a note to Government that "in her view it would be most unwise for Government to accede to this request as the organisation might waste the money."

This information led to my resolve to organize a

protest at Parliament and lodge a case with the Waitangi Tribunal. Both Awanuiarangi and Raukawa were initially unsupportive of this of action. Awanuiarangi said they could not afford to go to Wellington and believed nothing could be achieved by protesting. Whata Winiata of Raukawa response was "e ki e Rongo is that what do you want to do?"

Undeterred I put the plan in operation to hikoi to Wellington. I sent Himiona of Awanuiarangi a note to book two buses and sent the account to Ngāti Awa Maori Trust Board. I personally paid for about fourteen more buses. Turoa Royal led Raukawa and we together had a very disciplined protest at Parliament with Hirini Meads speaking for Awanuiarangi. I don't remember seeing Wira Gardiner there.

When we lodged the Waitangi Tribunal Claim WAI 718 for urgency we jumped 600 places in the queue. The Waitangi Tribunal found in our favour that each Wananga be given sufficient capital to bring building facilities up to the standard of other tertiary institutions in New Zealand.

National Government were still in power when Bill Birch offered us $10 million. I stood up and said, "Well, I think we should go back to court." Needless to say we declined National's generosity and when Labour was subsequently elected to power, we began negotiations again, this time with Trevor Mallard. He was in a much more generous mood, "we will give you $40 million Rongo!" My response was, "No Minister, we believe the minimum should be $60 million." I knew that several universities had received many more times that figure in capital over the years and even my economic advisors said $60 million for TWOA was far too low!

I guess in frustration, Trevor suddenly said "OK, $60 million it is, but we will start at $40 million and the other $20 million will be dependent on student numbers." OK was our response, how many students? Trevor came back with a number he thought we would never reach, around 11,000 EFTS by 2003, that is 8,000 more than we had achieved to date. With our teaching innovations, by 2003 we achieved 34,000 EFTS three times the target Trevor Mallard set. Then in 2005 the Government decided under political pressure to renege on the final $20 million capital instalment "calling it bad management by Rongo Wetere." The rest is history.

It is now 30 years since Joe Arrell, Buck Nin, I and others decided we wanted to build an institution to make a *real difference* in Aotearoa New Zealand. For this we are proud. It should be noted that in 2005, the Waitangi Tribunal (WAI 1298) recommended that the Crown formally acknowledge the invaluable and innovative contribution made by the Aotearoa Institute, and Dr. Rongo Wetere, from Ngāti Maniapoto, the founders of Te Wānanga o Aotearoa.

This account by Dr. Bruce Bryant, *A Small Window*, explains in full the events which led to state takeover of Te Wananga o Aotearoa in 2005. I am grateful to Bruce who on his own accord was motivated to write his personal account in an endeavour to set the record straight. His efforts are an absolute contrast to some members of TWOA Council who by their silence and lack of support for Aotearoa Institute and myself, are hard to understand or comprehend. The Trustees of Aotearoa Institute have been unwavering in their support, and my inspiration to keep going to build a life after TWOA. I hope that those who read *A Small Window* can appreciate that even after several years, a small window can reveal so much.

I am appreciative of the contents of a letter sent to the chair of Aotearoa Institute by the Hon Steven Joyce, Minister of Economic Development, Science and Innovation, Tertiary Education, Skills and Employment, and Associate Minister of Finance, dated 29 August 2012. Key statements made by the Minister were:

- "The Government wishes to express its thanks to the Aotearoa Institute and the founding communities of Te Wānanga o Aotearoa, for their innovative and invaluable contribution to education in Aotearoa New Zealand".
- "The Government acknowledges the constituents of the founding collective of Te Wānanga o Aotearoa, led by Dr Rongo Wetere and supported by Ngāti Maniapoto and the Aotearoa Institute".
- "The Government recognises that Aotearoa Institute, as the parent body from which Te Wānanga o Aotearoa developed, has made an important contribution to the tertiary education system".

- "Te Wānanga o Aotearoa and the Aotearoa Institute through Dr Rongo Wetere have supported indigenous education in an international context, hosting participation in the *World Indigenous Peoples Conference on Education* (WIPEC) in 2005. Te Wānanga o Aotearoa was also instrumental in the establishment of the *World Indigenous Nations Higher Education Consortium* (WINHEC) in 2002".

I am sure that we made a difference".

Postscript

There is more to this story that might help you to understand the political machinations of the state. Dr Wetere had been a long time member of the National Party and during 2003- 2004 was approached to put his name forward for the position of National Vice-President Māori. This was at a time when the Labour Party was in power. As you may have noted, it may be ironic that Dr Wetere's dealings with National for capital funding of wānanga, were unsuccessful, and it was not until Labour came to power in 1990, that any positive progress was made.

However, as you have seen, all was not well for TWOA in Wellington from as early as 2002, with Minister Mallard wrongly accusing the "bastards" at TWOA of "taking $600 million of unbudgeted expenditure"; Mallard having McNally appointed as a Labour Party watchdog to the TWOA Council, Mallard's signals for the reintroduction of the cap to tertiary enrolments, which clearly were aimed at restricting growth at TWOA, and his threat to academic freedom by suggesting legislation to limit Wananga enrolments to Māori only.

Following the Orewa speech January 2004 by the then leader of the National Party, Don Brash, and the ensuing debates that followed, Dr Wetere and others decided that it was probably time to consider the formation of a new political party. The discussions were about a party that could include representations to more accurately reflect the changing face of Aotearoa New Zealand. Several meetings were held around the country, which attracted attention. As a result, Dr Wetere became well known for his view that Māori should join with Pacific Islanders and migrant communities to form a new vision for Aotearoa New Zealand and at the time, there were many discussions at these meetings about the formation of a Māori party.

At the same time, discontent was apparent in the Labour Party as a result of a court judgment on the ownership of the foreshore and seabed. This led to the resignation of a Labour Party Member, Tariana Turia, who then went on to form the Māori Party in July 2004.

I know that Dr Wetere shared his views regarding a new vision for Aotearoa New Zealand with a person who was at the time looking for a political career with the Labour Party. I, and those with whom I associate, have little doubt that this person passed Dr Wetere's political aspirations on to the then Prime Minister. The person subsequently became a Labour Party politician.

In 2009, a senior partner of Price Waterhouse Coopers in Aotearoa New Zealand told me that the state attacks on TWOA and Dr Wetere were "ordered by the Prime Minister, directed by the Prime Minister's Private Secretary, and carried out by the Minister of Education". In view of this person's fellow partner's involvement with TWOA, Roache, I conclude that this is what actually happened.

The actions of the state against Dr Wetere as I have

described in this narrative, not only gave the state control of TWOA to resize as they wished, but by discrediting Dr Wetere as they did, also neutralised a potentially powerful political opponent.

Finally, it is my belief that the record should be set straight as to what the founders and those who worked so hard to build TWOA, had in mind. Although Aotearoa Institute was set up to enhance educational opportunities for Māori, TWOA resulted from the Education Amendment Act 1990, which describe wananga as:

"A wānanga is characterised by teaching and research that maintains, advances, and disseminates knowledge and develops intellectual independence, and assists the application of knowledge regarding āhuatanga Māori (Māori tradition) according to tikanga Māori (Māori custom)".

What the Act did not say, was that wānanga is exclusively for Māori, nor for the delivery of Māori only studies. Custom and tradition are just that. They make up the richness that societies build into their respective cultures. One thing that I believe that colonisation did, was to deny that there was any merit in the cultures of indigenous peoples, despite the fact, that with any degree of empathy, it must have been apparent to even the most blind, that there was so much to be learned from them. I do not think that any culture is better than any other, and that there are good and bad in most. However, after nearly a thousand years of living in Aotearoa New Zealand, without I remind you, televisions, telephones, and vehicles, surely provided to Māori, a huge understanding of what worked and perhaps did not work for them, and for the country, generally.

Those at TWOA were never interested in separatism. In reality, there was always an even balance between Māori and non-Māori in all aspects of TWOA, be it governance, management or teaching staff, and by 2003, in student profiles. Some of the real contributors to the development of TWOA came from outside of Aotearoa New Zealand, attracted as many Pākehā were, to the warmth and feeling of collectiveness that āhuatanga Māori and tikanga Māori are all about. My view is that the fact that only 49% of students were by 2004, Māori, was a massive testament to what TWOA was, and was a distinction that should have been celebrated as a major step forward in the development of our multi-cultural society. In a very short time, Aotearoa New Zealand will be able to boast being one of the most multi-cultured societies in the world, but I am not sure that as a country, we are very well prepared for this.

I suspect that an opportunity has been lost to truly use what āhuatanga Māori and tikanga Māori can teach us all, in assisting to developing a far more compassionate place for all into the future.

A further thought. TWOA knew that the growth that it achieved up 2003, was not sustainable. 2004 saw a stabilisation at around 29,000 EFTS, down from the 2003 figure of 34,500. During 2004, the strategic planning process identified a vision at about 30,000 EFTS annually, understanding that student numbers were likely to reduce in the foundation courses, but it was envisaged that students would then move on to degree courses, either with TWOA, or with another institution. TWOA, aware of their limitations, was in dialogue with Waikato University, at a governance level, with the possibility of some sort of partnership/merger on the table. The state of course, put pay to this.

About the author

I consider that I was somewhat privileged to be brought up in Te Awamutu, a small rural town in the Waikato province of Aotearoa New Zealand, said by many to be the home of some of the best dairy land in the world. I concede that privilege relates to the fact that it was a small town, very rural in outlook, with great schooling, and generally far away from the woes of the world. Te Awamutu can boast some very proud sons and daughters, including; a President of the Law Commission, several Queen's/Senior Counsel, internationally recognised - heart and cancer researchers, internationally recognised musicians and sports people, a Rhodes Scholar, senior business leaders, and just what I generally call, a lot of very decent people.

That privilege had a fair bit to do with the fact that I am Pākehā; that is, a European New Zealander, born in Aotearoa New Zealand to an English Mum and an Australian Dad, making me a first generation Kiwi. Many of my school friends, I belatedly found out (when I was 10 years old in fact, being taught New Zealand history at the time. Prior to this, I didn't really notice that we had slightly different coloured skins!) were Māori, who again, as I was belatedly to find out, were not as privileged as some of us Pākehā. The New Zealand history being taught at the time (of course) was written by the victors, as history tends to be and the plight of my Māori colleagues, past and current, was not really a topic for discussion.

As a matter of interest, five people named Bryant were amongst the original 'guests' of the first fleet to Australia that I referred to in the Introduction: Ann, for theft of muslin; John for assault; Michael, for 'stealing' a 'gentleman's' coat (the Old Bailey transcripts suggest that the said 'gentleman' lost his coat 'while under the influence'); Thomas for highway robbery, and then William for forgery. William went on to marry Mary, who became the famous Mary Bryant (Bryant, Mary b.1765). Quite a skill set these Bryant people brought to the colony! I cannot say with absolute authority that the above were part of my family, but the ingrained republican and socialist tendencies of generations of my Australian family, would suggest they might have been. Another thing, my grandfather on Dad's side was William, and two of my Aussie cousins are John and Michael! Life wasn't easy for these 'convicts', but neither was it in their home country for the great masses that they were forced to leave behind. All character building stuff that no doubt it has something to do with the deep feelings of resentment I hold for oppression of people on any level.

You might ask why a Pākehā (white boy) would wish to take up this challenge on behalf of Māori. In the first instance, I don't think that the underlying, 'real' issues relate only to Māori; I think that they relate to the abuse of political power. No one is immune from a corrupt political process and if the people cannot trust the political system, why should they commit to it? (An example is the French Revolution - horrible, but the people spoke). Secondly, there was certainly a race issue here, and nothing disgusts me more than the claim to racial superiority. As far as race is concerned, this is an evolutionary fact, which as a consequence has brought to us the wonders of differences in cultures, and adds to the excitements of being human.

I was appalled by the actions of the state and those they employed to assist them and I wished their actions to be recorded. My key focus however was to ensure that I was as objective as possible in how I told this story. I therefore decided to start this journey with a doctoral thesis studying two significant events that faced Waikato Māori: first, the introduction of the New Zealand Settlement Act 1863 and second, the state's battle for control of TWOA. Both of these events had detrimental outcomes for Māori of the Waikato. I The reason for the link back to the 1863 Act was that the state's role in 1863 and 1864 were well documented, as to reasons, methods used and outcomes; whereas very little had been written about TWOA's dealings with the state. I hope that academic rigour took any bias out of the thesis.

My conclusions were that both events I examined were constructed by colonial and post colonial powers. Both were abuses of that power. In my opinion, the 1863 Act was designed only to transfer to settlers' ownership, land confiscated by the settler government after an army invasion; and the other, to obtain control of TWOA. Both events were economically driven for the benefit of one sector of the population in favour of the other, by what were and still are for the most part, settler controlled and dominant governments. Rather than boring you to tears about the land issues of 1863, I have left this extensive section of my original thesis out of this narrative to concentrate on the TWOA injustice.

There is some degree of providence in my journey. It starts with a chance meeting with Dr Wetere (not then Doctor) in the main street of Te Awamutu in 1979 that lead to my role as a Trustee of Aotearoa Institute in 1988. This institute passed over its activities to the newly created Te Wānanga o Aotearoa in 1993, where I became a Ministerial appointed Councillor. I sat at that table until early 2005, as a Councillor for ten years, and as an advisor for two. Over seventeen years; I heard, learnt and saw a lot.

What a journey! To be part of this creation was a privilege: watching highly talented and inspirational people build a huge tertiary educational institute, completely within government policies of the day, and contributing to the 'knowledge economy' which was so often virtuously hailed as the economic wisdom of the late 1990s, early twenty first century. To witness the reputational assassination of Dr Wetere, was simply horrible, and if by publishing this account, his reputation can be restored, I will have had achieved my objective.

Translations

Āhuatanga Māori	Māori tradition
Aroha	Love
Hapū	Sub-tribe
Hīkoi	Step Out. March
Hui	Meeting
Iwi	Tribe
Kaitiaki	Guardian
Karakia	Prayer
Kaumatua	Elder
Kaupapa	Philosophy
Kawanatanga	Government
Kingitanga	Kingship
Kōkiri	Enterprise
Korowai	Cloak
Kura	School
Mana	Integrity, charisma, prestige.
Māori	Indigenous people of Aotearoa New Zealand.
Marae	Meeting area
Matauranga	Knowledge
Ngāti	A word preceding an Iwi name.
Ngāti Maniapoto	Iwi of the Taranaki and Waikato regions of Aotearoa New Zealand.
Pākehā	A non-Māori person.
Pōwhiri	Welcome

Rangātiratanga	Autonomy, self determination.
Tapu	Sacred
Tauira	Student
Te Reo Māori	Māori language
Tikanga Māori	Māori custom
Taonga	Treasure
Tohunga	Expert
Tumuaki	Chief executive
Waka	Canoe
Wānanga	Learning, a series of discussions
Whakairo	Carving
Whakapapa	Genealogy
Whare	House
Whānau	Extended family

Figures

Figure 1

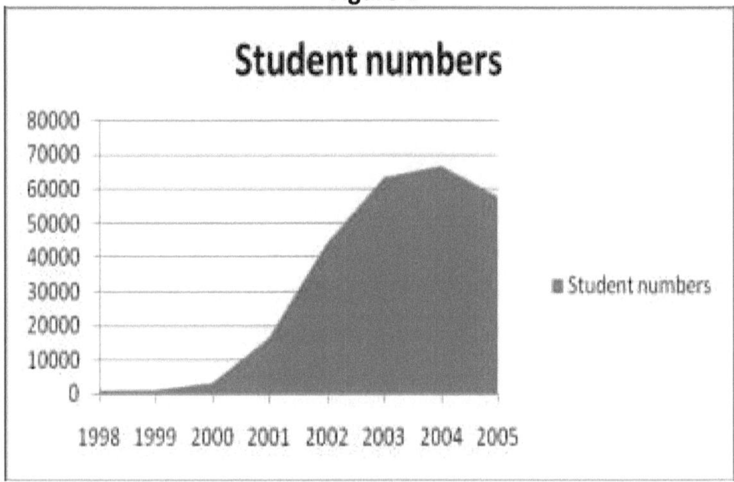

Figure 2

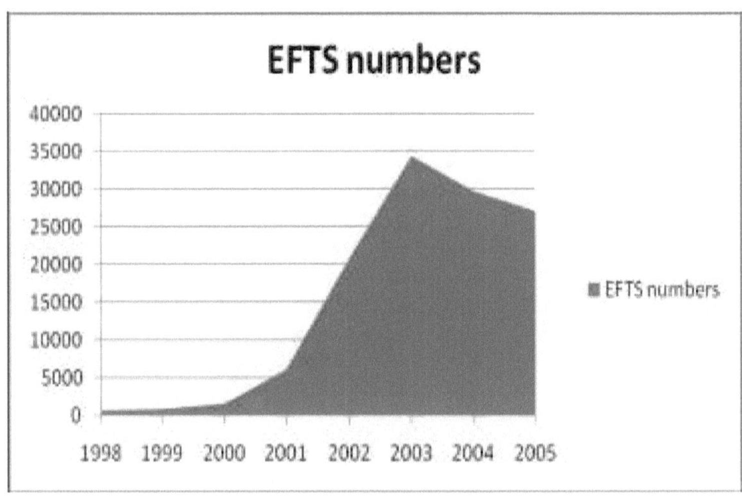

Figure 3
Student fees $

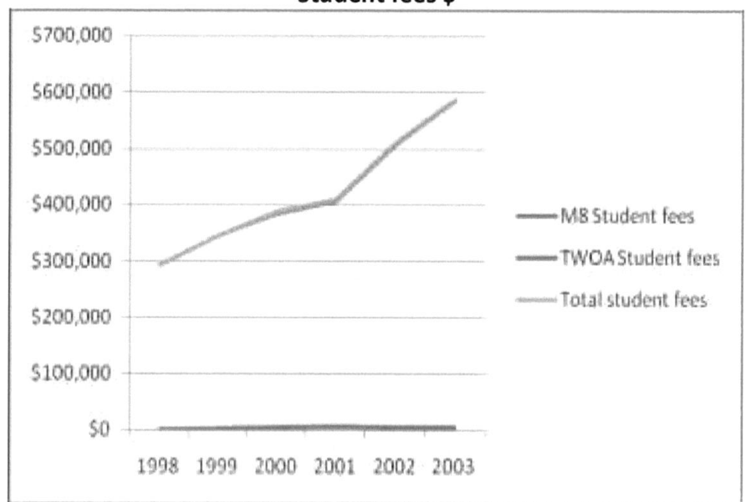

M8 is the eight universities

Figure 4
EFTS Funding $

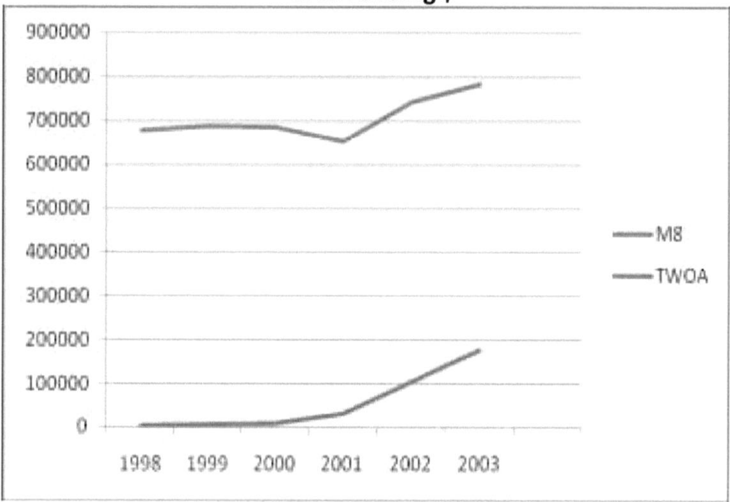

M8 is the eight universities

Figure 5
Student numbers

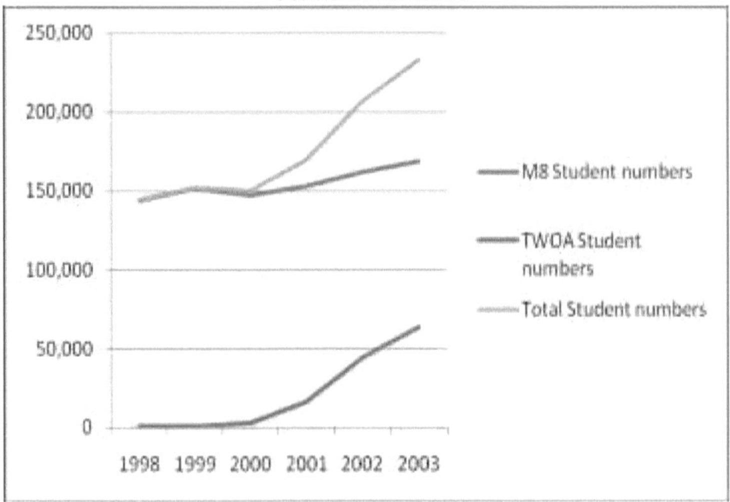

M8 is the eight universities

Figure 6
EFTS numbers

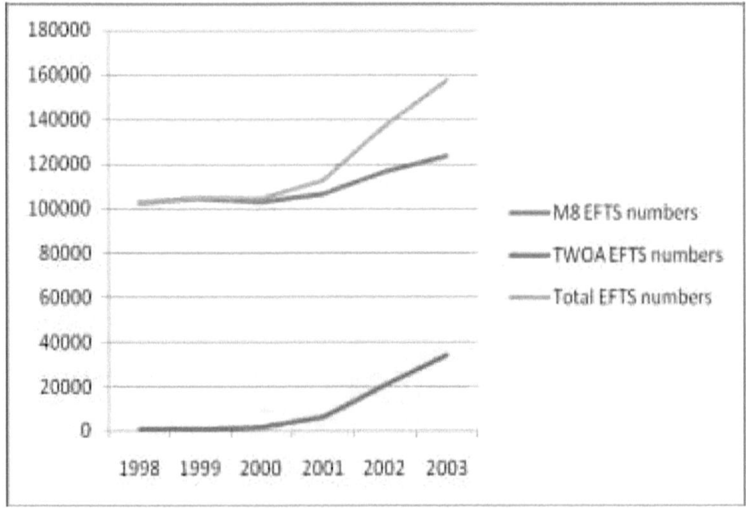

M8 is the eight universities

Tables

Table 1: Sector analysis 1998 ($, 000,000)

	2	3	4	5	6	7	8
	EFTS$	S/F$	Rev$	Exes$	Surplus$	EFTS#	SF#
Auckland Uni	$160	$62	$311	$299	$2	21	26
AUT	$49	$22	$101	$94	$6	10	24
Canterbury	$77	$29	$126	$130	($4)	11	12
Lincoln	$20	$10	$58	$55	($0.2)	3	3
Massey	$114	$47	$209	$197	$12	17	32
Otago	$110	$55	$264	$247	$17	14	16
Victoria	$74	$30	$130	$128	$2	11	13
Waikato	$67	$33	$135	$127	$7	10	12
Total Unis	$675	$293	$1,338	$1,280	$44	102	143
SF to EFT	43.39%						
TWOA	$3,	$0.8	$5	$5	$.005	0.7	0.9
TWOA % T Unis	0.46%	0.29%	0.41%	0.42%	0.11%	0.68%	0.64%
Total of Group	$678	$293	$1,344	$1,286	$44	103	144
TWOA %	0.46%	0.29%	0.41%	0.42%	0.11%	0.67%	0.64%

Note: Red (brackets) denotes loss/deficit: SF is Student fees. Blue: TWOA, for clarity purposes.

Table 2: Sector analysis 2001 ($, 000,000)

	2	3	4	5	6	7	8
	EFTS$	**S/F$**	**Rev$**	**Exes$**	**Surplus$**	**EFTS#**	**SF#**
Auckland Uni	$168	$96	$416	$406	$10	24	29
AUT	$6	$31	$125	$119	$3	10	24
Canterbury	$73	$31	$149	$153	($4)	10	11
Lincoln	$17	$12	$60	$60	($0.8)	2	3
Massey	$129	$78	$269	$255	$15	19	37
Otago	$122	$71	$304	$284	$19	15	17
Victoria	$69	$36	$143	$137	$5	12	15
Waikato	$62	$47	$147	$142	$4	10	13
Total Unis	**$651**	**$405**	$1,615	$1,559	$54	106	152
SF to EFT%		**62.77%**					
TWOA	$30	$5	$37	$35	$2	6,118	16
TWOA %	4.64%	1.39%	2.33%	2.29%	3.46%	5.76%	10.77%
TWOA%	**4.44%**	**1.37%**	2.28%	2.24%	3.34%	5.45%	9.72%

Note: Red (brackets) denotes loss/deficit: SF: is Student fees. Blue: TWOA, for clarity purposes.

Table 3: Sector analysis 2003 ($, 000,000)

	2	3	4	5	6	7	8
	EFTS$	S/F$	Rev$	Exes$	Surplus $	EFTS#	SF#
Auckland Uni	$191	$134	$505	$490	$15	27	33
AUT	$76	$67	$168	$161	$6	15	25
Canterbury	$80	$61	$173	$170	$3	12	12
Lincoln	$15	$23	$60	$59	$1	3	4
Massey	$136	$118	$328	$312	$14	22	41
Otago	$139	$79	$330	$324	$6	16	18
Victoria	$82	$37	$182	$175	$16	14	18
Waikato	$60	$61	$176	$168	$8	11	14
Total Unis	$782	$584	$1,926	$1,861	$71	123	169
SF to EFT		74.80%					
TWOA	$177	$3	$187	$154	$33	34	63
TWOA	22.64%	0.56%	9.74%	8.30%	46.33%	27.78%	37.51%
TWOA	18.46%	0.56%	8.88%	7.66%	31.66%	21.74%	27.28%

Note: SF: is Student fees. Red: used for emphasis. Blue: TWOA, for clarity purposes.

Table 4: Summary of financial data ($, 000,000

	1998	1999	2000	2001	2002	2003
Total unis EFTS	**$675**	**$686**	**$684**	**$651**	**$741**	**$782**
TWOA EFTS	$3	$4	$7	$30	$103	$177
Total EFTS	**$678**	**$690**	**$692**	**$681**	**$845**	**$959**
Total unis S fee	**$293**	**$344**	**$385**	**$405**	**$507**	**$584**
TWOA S fee	$0.8	$2	$4	$5	$3	$3
Total S fee	**$293**	**$346**	**$389**	**$411**	**$511**	**$588**
Total unis EFTS	**102**	**104**	**103**	**106**	**116**	**123**
TWOA EFTS	0.7	0.9	1	6	20	34
Total EFTS	**103**	**105**	**104**	**112**	**136**	**157**
Total unis Stud #	**143**	**150**	**146**	**152**	**161**	**169**
TWOA Stud #	0.9	1	3	16	44	63

Note: - S fee: is Student fees. Blue: TWOA, for clarity purposes.

www.ingramcontent.com/pod-product-compliance
Ingram Content Group UK Ltd.
Pitfield, Milton Keynes, MK11 3LW, UK
UKHW041946190726
13854UKWH00004B/1817